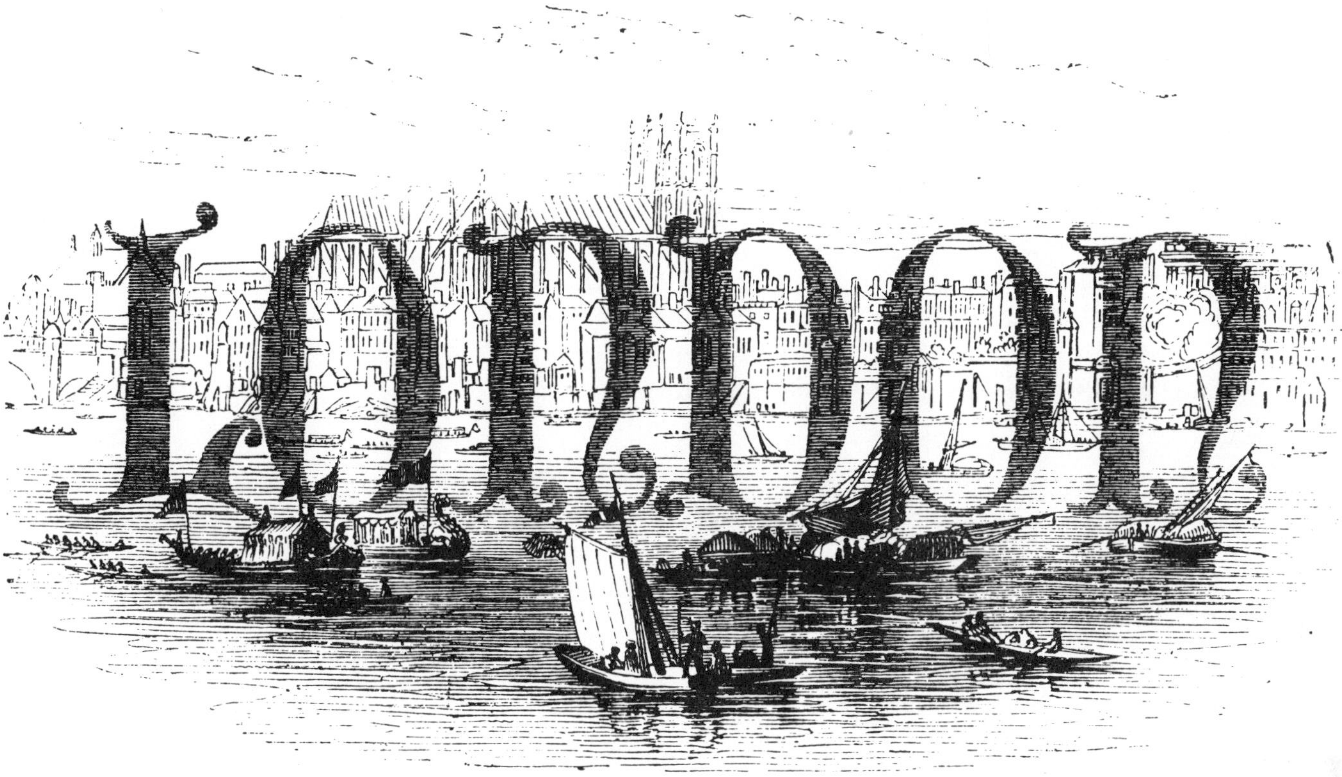

A look at London through Victorian eyes

Much controversy has been aroused through the Prince of Wales's call for a retention of the classical London skyline created by Wren and continued through the Georgian and Victorian period of London's growth. Charles Knight, publisher, author and innovator of numerous literary and artistic projects including 'the Penny Magazines' commissioned the best of London's artists of early Victorian times to illustrate the London he knew and loved so much. From these splendid illustrations and writings we can see and experience the scenes that Prince Charles believes that we have lost forever.

Through the brilliance of Charles Knight's artists we can see what was London and is London no more. Extracts from Charles Knight's six volumes of LONDON published in 1840 add a true authenticity to the engravings. Churches and buildings destroyed – sometimes by wartime blitz, fire and on many occasions by developers not only of today but of Victorian times as well. Who would believe that a wonderful Wren building only a short distance from St. Paul's degenerated into a butchers warehouse and was then demolished in 1847 – or that the splendour of the design of Brunel's first ever underwater tunnel would within 20 years of its opening become blackened with the filth of the steam trains of the London and Brighton Railway.

These are but a few of the unknown facts and scenes researched and depicted by the author of this book. It tells the story of London as it has never been told before. Furthermore through a facsimile of an 1837 edition of the 'Penny Magazine' it begins to tell the story of England and Europe as seen through the eyes of Charles Knight's early Victorian artists and correspondents. This was an era before photography had developed as a means of recording a visual moment in time. The boxwood engraving process was an art in itself and many of the artists and engravers whose superb works are recreated in this book exhibited at the Royal Academy and the Royal Society of Arts.

Charles Knight's London

First Published in England in 1990 by

STOW'S CLASSICS
HISTORIC GIFTWARE
NEWHAVEN FORT
NEWHAVEN
EAST SUSSEX

ISBN 1 872499 007

Printed in England by RAM Press Ltd, Newhaven, East Sussex.
Typesetting by Heather Mantell, Lewes, East Sussex.
Lithographic Reproduction by G.W. Litho Ltd, Hurstpierpoint, West Sussex.

Dedication

Writing this book and the development of the Charles Knight Collection of pictures, cards and other ideas for our range of historic giftware would not have been possible without the help, encouragement and endurance of my wife Wendy. I therefore dedicate this book to her in gratitude of her understanding and effort that has been necessary to reach its completion.

To the many others who have helped I thank most sincerely and in particular our daughter Tracy who has undertaken the laborious task of proof reading and associated critical analysis so vital to this type of project.

* * *

To the Reader

Many books have been written about London and it is extraordinary that someone with the genius and perception of Charles Knight should be the forgotten personality, when it was he who was the pioneer of mass production methods for illustrative journalism. He was an author, publisher and mass communicator who was the first to bring high quality weekly journals to the early Victorians in their quest for Knowledge.

Enjoy the scenes depicted by the superb artists that Charles Knight employed, read the fascinating history and then go out and about London and see what still remains of Charles Knight's London.

* * *

CHARLES KNIGHT.

Foreword

by

SIMON HUGHES
Liberal Democrat MP for Southwark and Bermondsey

When you are the latest MP in a series that started in 1285, you should be very conscious of history. When you are the MP for a place like Southwark & Bermondsey – on the main road from London to the rest of Europe, deep in archaeology, and rich in buildings, colour, drama and excitement – hardly a week passes without history intervening on to the agenda of today. And when your back yard and office are the great cities of London and Westminster, not a day goes past without a new revelation of site or fact about the great web of endeavour which created one of the greatest cities of the world.

And that was all without being introduced to the fascinating pen and perceptive eye of the great Charles Knight. Great – but far too obscured from recent memory. The bicentenary of Charles Knight's birth approaches fast. This amazing man – historian, writer, publisher, editor, scholar, educator, reformer, critic and commentator, a real man of letters – made a unique and hugely diverse contribution to London over a large part of the nineteenth century.

Derek Stow is determined to make sure we do not forget this. And that we discover or rediscover, appreciate, learn from and enjoy the work of someone who was indisputably an artist and innovator of particular note.

Derek Stow's book is the key to the door of a special understanding of life in Victorian London. Charles Knight's infectious enthusiasm has been passed on to Derek Stow and has now been passed equally infectiously to me. I hope many people will gain from this book not just a glimpse which illustrates so much of the past of London today, but a sense of the continuing history of which we are all custodians. Charles Knight and Derek Stow help us fulfil our obligation to ensure that London continues to enrich thousands and millions of lives.

This book is an education, a revelation and an inspiration. Thank you both.

Simon

House of Commons
Westminster

July 1990

Contents

Charles Knight's London

Preface

In the research and compilation of CHARLES KNIGHT'S OLD LONDON COLLECTION I have taken many unexpected twists and turns. For instance when I first came across the magnificent engravings which you can now enjoy in this book, I had no idea from where they originated nor was I aware of the enormous contribution that Charles Knight had made to the development of the learning concept of early Victorian times. I am therefore in considerable gratitude to the many people who have helped and contributed to my efforts to bring to everybody's awareness the work of the extraordinary man of charm and genius – CHARLES KNIGHT.

Whilst working at The County Hall London between 1983 and 1989 I was fortunate to have on hand the expertise, knowledge and advice of the Archivists and Librarians of the London Historical Records Office. They were a tremendous help and set me on the track of many aspects relating to the remarkable Charles Knight.

I am also grateful to the staff of the Corporation of London, particularly at the London Museum for their cooperation with our project at Stow's Classics whereby we processed the splendid original engravings into the 18 high quality framed pictures that are now on sale and form the CHARLES KNIGHT OLD LONDON COLLECTION.

Thanks are due also to Patrick Marrin of Marrin's Antiquarian Books for finding the original rare volumes for me to use during my research and add to my own collection of books on Old London. He also assisted with the detail on printing processes and general historical aspects.

It was a great pleasure to have the encouragement and support of the Windsor Express which was established by Charles Knight and his father in 1812. Francis Batt helped to trace some of the Windsor people who have striven for many years to ensure that their famous townsman receives the recognition that he so rightly deserves. Gordon Cullingham was formerly Borough Surveyor at Windsor and is now President of the Windsor Local History Group and welcomed the fact that Charles Knight's bicentenery would receive worldwide coverage through the recreating of the illustrations and writings.

It was also a wonderful experience to talk to 85 year old Lesley Lightfoot who was in the newspaper business for over 60 years – many of those years spent with the Windsor Express. He still has a regular column on Royal and Local History and it was most gratifying to have the help of a person who remembers the activities of 'The Batchelors of Windsor' – originally a Whig Reformist organisation – whom Charles Knight supported so strongly.

In paying full tribute to the man who originated the whole concept of popular illustrative journalism in the 1830's I am grateful to two organisations who help to preserve our historic past. The Mansell Collection permitted us to include the portrait of CHARLES KNIGHT which appears at the front of this book. The Illustrated London News have enabled us to provide a fitting ending to the book by allowing the inclusion of Charles Knight's Obituary which appeared in the ILN on 22 March 1873.

The year 1991 will be the bicentenary of the birth of CHARLES KNIGHT. We have launched the book and the pictures one year in advance in order that everybody has a chance to appreciate the work of a man who in the past has not been properly recognised for the contribution which he made to journalism, general education and printing processes.

January 1990 — Derek Stow

Introduction

RESTORATION OF THE ANCIENT THOROUGHFARE FROM WESTMINSTER TO LONDON.

Charles Knight's London

Introduction

It seems extraordinary that the name of Charles Knight has diminished into insignificance, considering the enormous contribution that he made to matters of historical, educational and general interest in the first half of the nineteenth century. He wrote prolifically – from his contributions as Founder of the Windsor and Eton Express in 1812 and later Editor and part owner of 'The Guardian' – to his autobiographical writings in his later life entitled 'Passages of a Working Life' and 'Shadows of Old Booksellers' which were published in the late 1860's.

However it was his 'Penny Magazines', London and Old England published between 1832 and 1845 which brought him the greatest public esteem during his lifetime. His aim was to bring the written word to 'the masses' and because such a large proportion of the children of the industrial revolution were illiterate, he believed that the right way to encourage people to learn about their heritage and the way of life in other countries was through high quality illustrations.

As the 'Penny Magazines' improved and the mass printing process became more viable he engaged some of the finest engravers in the country to illustrate his journals and books. The principal contributor to the improvement in the standard of illustrations was John Jackson, an apprentice and pupil of the famous Newcastle engraver Thomas Bewick who preferred to cut on the block from dark to light with an absence of the previous practice of cross hatching.

In 1834 Charles Knight appointed John Jackson as his Chief Engraver who, with assistants S. Sly and J. Wilson, invented a process whereby the superb drawings could be recreated with skill and precision; then most vital of all, be turned into stereotypes yet still retain the quality and integral beauty of the artist's original work. The engravings reproduced in this book and the quality giftware items which are now available from 'Stow's Classics' Charles Knight Collection are the result of these skills.

The age of commercial photography was still a long way off and it was around the time that Charles Knight engaged these top London artists to illustrate his London books and periodicals that the Frenchman Dageurre and Englishman William Fox Talbot first developed a negative. It was not until the 1890's that such pictures could be processed onto ordinary paper and the high quality engravings of the 1840's were therefore a great attraction and the only visual record available of places, people and events.

Throughout the nineteenth century the wood block illustration and its various means of stereotyping became a feature of mass journalism. It was a matter of 'every picture tells a story' and it was this feature that Charles Knight emphasised. It acted as the photograph does today and we can therefore see for ourselves delightful buildings and bridges that no longer exist and scenes which are a genuine reminiscence of Victorian times. Charles Knight's London contained some of the finest pictures but many of his other journals are illustrated with scenes throughout Britain and Europe although Knight himself was not a great traveller. It was his vision and editorial skills that make his works so vitally invaluable today when it is considered by many people that much of the City of London is being devastated by the 'Developers' of a so called modern age.

Illustration on Page 2.

View of Old London, looking eastward from the Strand. On the left foreground is the entrance to Covent Garden; on the right the rookery of Durham House; onward the Palace of the Savoy; the Strand Inn; the Temple; to Blackfriars; Castle Baynard; Old St. Paul's, &c.; London Bridge. On the Surrey side – St. Mary Overies; Bishop of Winchester's Palace, &c.

Artist W.H. Pyne. Engraver John Jackson.

Our emphasis on the beauty and intrinsic value of the 'Boxwood Engraving era' should not detract from the high quality of writing and descriptive narrative contained in Charles Knight's publications. The vivid scene in 'The Silent Highway' – the first chapter of his six volume book on 'London' has few counterparts:

> We have stood for a few moments on the eastern side of London Bridge, looking upon that sight which arrests even the dullest imagination – mast upon mast, stretching further than the eye can reach, the individual objects constantly shifting, but the aggregate ever the same.
>
> We pass to the western side and descend the steps of the bridge. We are in a narrow and dirty street but we look up to the magnificent land arch which crosses it. A turn to the left brings us to the river. A bell is ringing; we pass through a toll gate paying four-pence and in a few seconds are on one of the little steam boats bearing poetical names of some flower, or planet, or precious gem.
>
> As the hand of the clock upon the pier approaches to one of the four divisions of the hour, the boat prepares to start. The pilot goes to the helm, the broad plank over which the passengers go is removed – the steam is up. For a minute we appear as if we were passing down river but, threading its way through a dozen other steam winged vessels, the boat darts to the Surrey shore and her prow is breasting the ebbing tide.
>
> What a gorgeous scene is now before us! The evening sun is painting the waters with glancing flames; the cross upon that mighty dome of St. Paul's shines like another sun; churches, warehouses, steam chimneys, shot towers, wharfs, bridges – the noblest and humblest things – all are picturesque; and the eye looking upon the mass, sees nothing of that meanness with which our Thames banks were once reproached.

These excursions and scenes of what Victorians treasured as their historic London were captured by the ingenious melding of literature and art. The value of Charles Knight's contribution to the development of a whole range of processes and ideas which improved our knowledge of English Heritage certainly warrants wider recognition.

He commented little on the traumatic developments and social evils that had evolved during the Industrial revolution but was in fact one of the original Whig reformists. It seemed the whole purpose of his life was to identify things of interest which should be brought to the attention of everybody not only for educational purposes but also enjoyment. We rely on television and radio; colour seems to be essential to us today; yet it was illustrative journalism and engravings of the Victorian Age that was their equivalent to the mass media hype of the 1990's.

Charles Knight pioneered the improvement in the quality of illustrative journalism and methods by which large scale production could occur whilst still maintaining high standards. Before 1820 illustrated periodicals in Great Britain were very rare. Some crude wood blocks had appeared in 'The Times' in 1806 but it was considered to be an 'expensive luxury'. However they installed a Konig steam power printing machine in 1814.

But the real impetus came from the tremendous demand for information which by the mid 1830's was escalating to such a degree, that a group of eminent people led by the Whig Reformist Lord Brougham, appointed Charles Knight as Publisher and initiator in the setting up of an organisation known as 'The Society for the Diffusion of Useful Knowledge' nick-named 'The Steam Intellect Society'. It was this body that stimulated Charles Knight into enormous activity and he produced a wide range of books and journals of outstanding variety and high quality. Of all Charles Knight's achievements it was the 'Penny Magazines' for which he was most widely known and respected but the extent of his writings was vast.

-Steam Printing Machine

He wrote his six volumes on 'London' (as the original edition was known) between 1835 and 1842 and they were released as 'weeklies' between 1841 and 1844. The title inscribed on the limited and updated version issued after his death by Virtue and Company was 'History of London'. This would certainly not have been to his liking because in the first edition in 1840 Charles Knight says in his introduction:

> This is a NEW WORK ON LONDON; and the principle which we have thus indicated of looking at the Present through the Past, and the Past through the Present, requires that our Work shall be wholly different from any that has preceded it. It will neither be a 'Survey' of London, nor a 'History of London'.
>
> Its arrangement will be neither topographical nor chronological. It will not travel 'with tedious steps and slow' from Portsoken Ward to Westminster nor begin with King Lud and end with Victoria ... The greatest and meanest features of a city lie mingled together, in the same way that the mightiest and minutest works of nature are presented to the observing eye.

This is how Charles Knight saw his London and he portrayed it throughout in this loving and caring way. He strove for perfection both in the written word and in the illustrations so that the 'masses' could see and know about their present circumstances and the past.

Throughout his six volumes on 'London' Charles Knight refers frequently to the work of other London historians and antiquarians – Fitzwilliam, Maitland, Strype, Pennant and above all the most revered was the sixteenth century antiquarian and chronicler John Stow. Knight comments:

> Few words spoken among men, have or ever had, so much significancy for the imagination as the word LONDON. Rarely has a single name been so full of meaning to so many minds, or been gifted with the power of awakening so many various trains of reflection...

Amongst the earliest investigators of London were the two chroniclers Fabian and Arnold. Fabian's Chronicles of 1485 contains various verses, narratives and soliloquies and sometime later in 1521 Arnold's 'Chronicle or Customs of London' was printed.

> Fabian and Arnold and after them Leland, Norden, Camden and others, all broke ground in different parts of the great field of the antiquities of London: but the first trudger and trencher in the field in its whole extent was the excellent John Stow ... indeed it was he who has supplied the most valuable part of every work that has since appeared calling itself a history or survey of London ...

John Stow was born in 1525 and died in 1605 thus encompassing the dramatic period in history of the reigns of Henry VIII, Elizabeth, Mary, James the First and the Cromwellian period. Favoured religions changed dependent on the Sovereign's wishes and this led Stow into some problems in 1568 when, as though he was under some form of suspicion, his collection of old manuscripts and books was brought to the notice of the Queen's Council. It was the 'fantastical old Popish books' which caused the problem. But John Stow lived a simple and somewhat poverished life following his trade as a Tailor and undertaking his research and antiquarian activitivies in his spare time.

Stow's Monument, in the Church of St. Andrew Undershaft.

He lived in London all his life 'near the Pump in Aldgate' but after witnessing a horrific execution in front of his own house he moved to Lime Street. In 1560 he produced his 'Summary of the Chronicles of England' and worked continuously on historical and antiquarian matters but it was almost 40 years later before he published his life long study of the history of London entitled 'A Survey of London' which he dedicated to the Lord Mayor of London. He received much thanks but little remuneration for his efforts but the City recognised the value of his work by placing a monument in the Church of St. Andrew Undershaft following his death in 1605. The monument can still be visited to this day.

THE

PICTURE

OF

LONDON

1819.

Hyde Park Corner.

LONDON.

PUBLISHED BY LONGMAN, HURST, REES, ORME & BROWN.

PATERNOSTER ROW.

A

SVRVAY OF LONDON.

Conteyning the Originall, Antiquity,
Increase, Moderne estate, and description of that City, written in the yeare 1598, by Iohn Stow Citizen of London.

Since by the same Author increased,
with diuers rare notes of Antiquity, and *published in the yeare,* 1603.

Also an Apologie (or defence) against the
opinion of some men, concerning that Citie, the greatnesse thereof.

VVith an Appendix, contayning in Latine
Libellum de situ & nobilitate Londini: Written by William Fitzstephen, in the raigne of Henry the second.

Imprinted by Iohn Windet, Printer to the honorable Citie of London.
1603.

The other major feature of Charles Knight's 'London' was the work of Sir Christopher Wren. As Stow gave London the story of its past Wren projected its architectural future. Even before the Great Fire of London in 1666 which destroyed most of the city including St. Paul's, Wren had submitted proposals for radical changes to roads and buildings. It was the fire that was the catalyst for his ideas and he was commissioned to undertake much of the rebuilding and planning of Central London. His first plan was rejected by the city Commissioners but later revised to satisfy the Authorities. Nevertheless he had constant criticism and competition particularly in relation to the total rebuilding of St. Paul's Cathedral. In all he designed 53 London Churches and many other palaces and buildings, the whole effect of which was imprinted on the London that Charles Knight loved, described and illustrated so well.

In the advent of illustrative journalism there seemed to be some strange notion that 'something illustrated was something juvenile'. Knight did not share this concept and illustrated his journals lavishly. His awareness of the needs of an ever increasing population was justified and sales of his magazines had risen to 200,000 by 1835 – a quite amazing figure at that time. It is interesting to note that previously the hand printing process made mass distribution impossible as only 200 copies could be produced each hour and only on one side of the paper.

Knight employed the best artists and researchers he could find and unlike many other publishers of the time, had a high opinion of his illustrators. He was the first publisher to publicise the names of both the artist and the engraver and these were listed in his journals – be it sometimes only by surname. Although we identify the artists in the same way in this book we have also added what biographical notes we can to assist in the identification of styles of the various artists and engravers.

Charles Knight used a large number of authors – he called them 'correspondents' – and in his generous manner he always indicates who prepared or wrote each chapter. The extracts already quoted are those of Charles Knight himself but the strong tone of his editorial control persists throughout the full six volumes of 'London'. To help readers to appreciate the style and detail contained in his original writings, short extracts are included and are indented to identify their origin.

There are some other facets to the extraordinary talents of Charles Knight which will no doubt be of interest. He could be perceived to be the perpetrator of the library system having first set up a 'Reading Society' in Windsor in 1810. A new small volume about London was published in 1819 and no doubt the 'Society' reviewed the book which was called THE PICTURE OF LONDON. The frontpiece reproduced on the facing page shows that by this time the quality of wood block engraving had reached a high standard. The artist and engraver of this splendid volume was James Grieg.

Whilst Charles Knight was still assisting his father in the Windsor bookshop he identified the need for what was later to be described as 'Popular Literature'. He suggested that 'Book Clubs' should be formed with an organisation of them set up throughout London and maybe extend throughout the country. Later in a 'Penny Magazine' in May 1844 he set out his views on the concept.

> The principle of voluntary association for the purchase of books has scarcely been called into action; and the reason is pretty obvious. The machinery by which such associations work is too cuprous ... all the complex contrivances of management is kept in the hands of a directing few ... if a collection of books were published at a sufficiently rapid rate and at so low a price then they could soon find themselves to be capable of being the foundation of a library ... a subscription of one penny a week by twelve individuals would place at their command fifty two volumes in the course of a year ... The books might form a permanent library.

It is significant that around the same time a young Anthony Panizzi was attempting to standardize the Library and reference system in the British Museum and was subsequently accredited with establishing the existing public lending library system and Knighted for his efforts.

Charles Knight's foresight and control relating to printing processes was also far reaching. He was one of the first to patent a method of colour illustration for popular literature and although maybe the effect of the original browns, reds and rusts is very basic to us today, it was nevertheless an amazing breakthrough in the 1830's. George Baxter, the Lewes Printer, Publisher and Bookseller was the first to patent a device for colour printing in 1835 but three years later Charles Knight registered his 'Patent Illuminated Printing Machine'. The preceding ten years of trial and development in all aspects of letterpress and other forms of printing in mass production terms had its problems.

The main difficulties he encountered were of a technical nature. However there was also a shortage of good wood engravers – most being employed on expensive books which were only seen by 'the few'. This was contrary to the beliefs of Knight and he expressed in one of his journals that it was a 'complete betrayal of what wood engraving was about' and that this fine art should be developed and improved for all to enjoy.

The letterpress process, used with such great effect by Charles Knight, involved letters or blocks being imprinted onto paper or other material by pressure of a hand operated machine. This process was obviously slow but the other problem was that the paper became slightly marked or dented. The stereotype process which was the vital element to produce long runs, involved the type being transferred to limestone in order that the illustration could be incorporated which resulted in a lack of crispness.

After extensive experiments with his staff and his printer, William Clowes, he eventually found that the end cuts of Box wood made the best wood blocks for the purpose. He used a cylindrical machine and the text and woodcuts were transcribed onto stereotyped plates using a strictly uniform application of ink. Even the hard box wood engravings wore out and often two or more blocks of the same engraving would be made. Close examination of the imprints will sometimes reveal splits in the wood.

The other development which assisted Charles Knight from a technical point of view was firstly the Steam press and later the evolvement of electrotype. Although by the 1830's there were machines capable of printing 16000 copies a day the quality of reproduced engravings was affected and they lost their clarity. John Jackson contributed to ever improving standards, particularly relating to the engravings and the subsequent precision of the reproduction from artist's original work. In one of the articles in the 'Penny Magazine' Charles Knight wrote:

> Without the very ingenious invention of the Stereotype Foundling in which great practical improvements have been made within the last few years, 'this little work' could not be printed in duplicate, which diminishes the expense.

Circulation and distribution were vital to the success of his ideas and such foresighted booksellers as W. H. Smith assisted in the success of the 'Penny Magazine' and other similar publications. The date was now 1844 and the railway age had transformed the transport system within a decade. Knight continues:

> The communication between the capital and the country, and between large towns in the country and villages, is now so perfect, that wherever there is a sufficient demand for any commodity there will be a supply ... The steam-boat upon the seas – the canal – the railway – the quick van – these as well as the stage-coach and mail place the 'Penny Magazine' within everybody's reach in the farthest part of the kingdom, as certainly as if he lived in London, and without additional cost.

The 'Penny Magazine' covered an enormous range of subjects and included a series called 'London Through the Looking Glass' from which the major volumes on London materialised. These articles typify Charles Knight's look at the relatively recent past and even today they make fascinating reading. A complete issue of the 'Penny Magazine' for 29 July 1837 and its monthly supplement are included at the end of this book.

Charles Knight himself was a convivial and likeable man of medium build and finely cut features. A person of extreme compassion and care, he always expressed his concern about the working conditions and plight of 'poor' people and through his publications and countrywide lecture tours he felt that he could enhance their lives.

He was born in 1791 at Windsor. His father was a bookseller, author and publisher and was twice Mayor of Windsor. He had a small but prestigious location immediately opposite the Castle and Royalty frequently came and browsed around the shop. Charles was only two years old when his mother died and following what he described as 'a very happy childhood' was apprenticed to his father at 14 years of age and having such an affiliation with journalism he made rapid progress.

Following his early achievements with the 'Reading Society', Windsor and Eton Express and the Guardian he established himself as a major publisher by 1824 when he originated and edited 'Knight's Quarterly Magazine' being based at the prestigious address of 7 Pall Mall East. The idea of a National library was always in his mind and he sought the support of major figures among the Parliamentary Reformist. Earlier he had founded the publication 'Plain Englishman' in which he wrote an article entitled 'Diffusion of Useful Knowledge. He managed to attract the attention of Lord Brougham and suggested the name would be appropriate for a Society with an educational publishing programme. Charles Knight subsequently became its publisher and superintendent.

During the mid 1820's finances did not always go well which caused him problems in his latter years as well. Things improved in the 1830's and as well as his publishing activities he wrote prolifically in his own right. His six volume LONDON which is the subject of this book, two vast illustrated volumes of OLD ENGLAND, A PICTORIAL BIBLE AND AN ILLUSTRATED Shakespeare (then written as Shakspere) were just a few of his contributions to the literary scene.

During the 1850's he became a literary critic as well as continuing his writings on Old England and the ways of life of his time. He also wrote some plays for the London stage and tried his hand at acting, appearing with his friends Charles Dickens and Wilkie Collins. He was widely acclaimed in America where the 'Penny Magazines' and many of his books were distributed throughout North America.

But he had his own critics – some doubting that he had got through to the 'masses' or whether in fact he had purely enhanced the knowledge of the upper and middle classes. Twenty years after his death a reviewer of books was comparing Knight's London to a more recent six volume book called 'Old and New London' compiled by George Thornbury and Edward Woolford. The observer wrote:

> "...Mr. Knight's LONDON of 1841 is a book of the past. His streets and his Cockneys – even those of Dickens – are of another generation – the like of which we know more ... and the figures are less familiar to our sight than Chinamen."

Despite this posthumous critique his contemporaries were full of admiration of all his achievements and it was sad that he felt forced to refuce the Award of Honorary Membership of the Historical Society of Great Britain due to his blindness and failing health. Even the portrait at the front of this book which was taken in 1867, after his sight had deteriorated, reflects this character. In his later years he lived mainly at Hampstead being described as having 'flowing white locks'.

He gradually withdrew from business after his sight failed during the early 1860's and died at his Surrey home in Addlestone on 9 March 1873. He was laid to rest at his beloved home town of Windsor close to 'Batchelor's Acre' and a short distance from the Knight's original shop in Castle Hill. Windsor recognised his achievements through various memorials in the town but the country to which he gave so much has never fully appreciated the extraordinary contribution that he made to educational and journalistic development.

This is but a short summary of a man of many and great achievements and a more detailed account is best left to the content of the Obituary which appeared in the Illustrated London News on 22nd March 1873. The notice is included at the end of this book as a tribute to the man who now almost 200 years from his birth enlightens us in exquisite words and delightful illustrations of Charles Knight's LONDON.

> The features of this wonderful city – physical and moral, present and antiquarian, if truly and strikingly presented, are to be looked upon with interest and curiosity, by the stranger as well as the citizen who daily hears the sound of Bow Bell.
>
> London is not England, as Paris is said to be to France; neither is she the head and England the body, as used to be set down, but she is so identified with the whole empire – she absorbs and returns again so much of the general prosperity – that what belongs to her belongs to all.

Landmarks

1. WREN'S TOWERS AND SPIRES
2. OLD ROYAL EXCHANGE
3. OLD CORN EXCHANGE
4. TOWER OF LONDON
5. THE CUSTOMS HOUSE
6. THE GENERAL POST OFFICE

The Charles Knight Collection

OLD LONDON

Landmarks Series – No. 1 Wren's Towers and Spires

1. ST. DUNSTAN'S IN THE EAST – Burnt out in Blitz of 1941. Spire rebuilt 1953 and ruins still stand surrounded by gardens.
2. ST. MAGNUS – Minor damage in 1941.
3. ST. BENET, GRACECHURCH STEET – Demolished in 1867 for road building.
4. ST. EDMUND THE KING – War damage in 1917 and 1941 now restored.
5. ST. MARGARET PATTENS – Undamaged except for replacement glass in windows.
6. ALLHALLOWS THE GREAT. Tower demolished in 1876. Church demolished 1894.
7. ST. MARY ABCHURCH – Damaged in the Blitz of 1940 and again later.
8. ST. MICHAEL CORNHILL – Undamaged
9. ST. LAWRENCE, JEWRY – Totally destroyed by German bombers in 1940. Rebuilt to original design in 1957.
10. ST. BENET FINK – Demolished in 1844 to make way for Royal Exchange.
11. ST BARTHOLOMEW BY THE EXCHANGE – Demolished to make way for City development in 1841.
12. ST. MICHAEL, QUEENHITHE – Demolished in 1876 for City building programme.
13. ST. MICHAEL ROYAL – Damaged by Flying Bomb in 1944. Restored 1968.
14. ST. ANTHOLIN, WATLING STREET – Taken down in 1874 to make way for Queen Victoria Street.
15. ST. STEPHEN, WALBROOK – Badly damaged by enemy action in 1941. Rebuilt 1955.
16. ST. SWITHIN, CANNON STREET – Totally destroyed in air raid in 1941.
17. ST. MARY-LE-BOW – Badly damaged by bombs in 1941. Fully restored in 1964.
18. CHRISTCHURCH, NEWGATE STREET – Totally destroyed in 1940 Blitz by German bombers. Tower and ruins remained. Spire rebuilt in 1959.
19. ST. NICHOLAS, COLE ABBEY – Destroyed in 1941 by enemy action. Restored in 1962.
20. ST. MILDRED, Bread Street – Destroyed by bombing in 1940.
21. ST. AUGUSTINE, WATLING STREET – Destroyed in 1941 by German air attack.
22. ST. MARY SOMERSET – Demolished in 1872 to make way for City development but tower remains.
23. ST. MARTIN, LUDGATE – Very little damage during the war.
24. ST. ANDREW BY THE WARDROBE – Completely gutted by incendiary bomb in 1940 but rebuilt in 1962.
25. ST. BRIDE'S, FLEET STREET – Destroyed by enemy bombing in 1940. Rebuilt in 1964.

*

Sir Christopher Wren planned and supervised the rebuilding of London Churches after the Great Fire of London in 1666. The churches in this Premier Reproduction in the Stow's Classics series were built between 1670 until Wren's death in 1723. St. Pauls Cathedral was his greatest achievement and despite some damage during the Second World War is now completely restored. The scale of the engraving is expressed precisely in relation to St. Pauls.

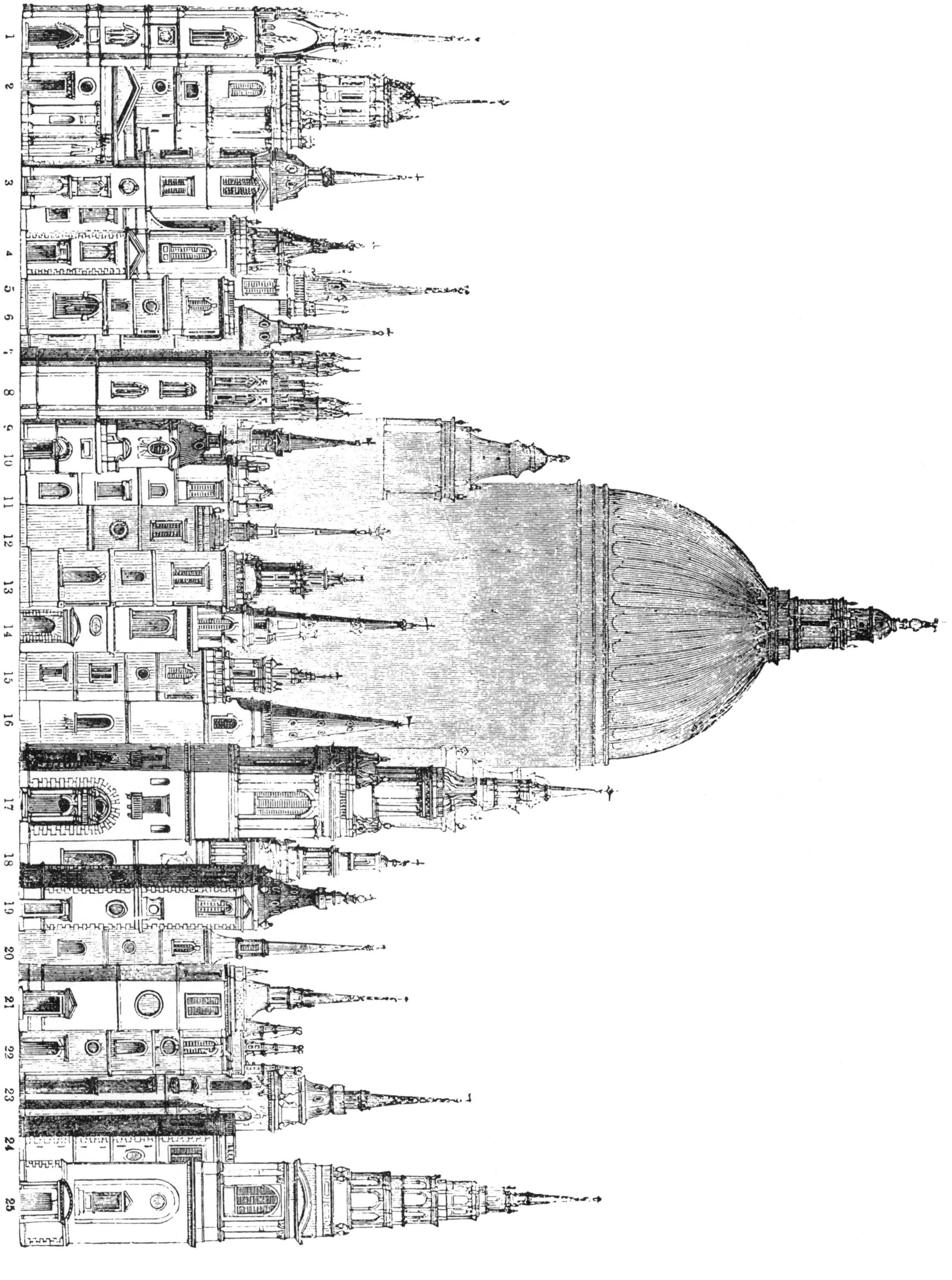
1
2
3
4
5
6
7
8
9
10
11
12
13
14
15
16
17
18
19
20
21
22
23
24
25

The Charles Knight Collection

OLD LONDON

Landmarks Series – No. 2 Old Royal Exchange

The original concept of a Royal Exchange was as the result of initiatives by Sir Richard Gresham who had been very much involved with the financial goings on of the City of London. During his year as Lord Mayor in 1537, he proposed the erection of a building in Lombard Street. It is however the name of Thomas, the younger of his two sons that London remembers as the founder of the Royal Exchange.

There was obviously a great need for such an establishment, John Stow, the famous London Historian observed in his Chronicles which were published in 1598, 'The merchants and tradesmen ... for the general making of bargains, contracts and commerce did meet twice on every day ... but the meetings were unpleasant and troublesome by reason of walking and talking in such a narrow street, being there constrained to endure all extremes of weather.'

The foundation stone of the first Royal Exchange was laid at the Cornhill location in June 1566 and the entire building was completed by November 1567. Disastrously it was totally destroyed in the Great Fire of London in 1666 but the rebuilding was undertaken quickly and the Architect, under the watchful eye of Christopher Wren, completed it to a similar style as the original building which was reopened in September 1669.

The second Royal Exchange which is the subject of this picture met the same fate as the first building. Charles Knight describes the scene.

> It was the night of Wednesday, the 10th of January, 1838... that from the windows of the nearby Lloyd's Coffee room that the flames first became visible to the watchmen and to the astonished merchants and others, who quickly came hurrying to the spot, only in time to behold the edifice perish by the same agency as its predecessor ... amidst the tumult of the populace, the shouts of the firemen, and the crashing of fallen masonry, the bells of the tower began to play their popular air and then to fall one after the other into the common ruin beneath.

The building which now stands on the same spot was designed by Tite being rebuilt between 1842 and 1844.

The artist of this fine drawing was Frederick Fairholt who won the Society of Arts award when he was just twenty years old. He was a scenic painter, illustrator and engraver although this engraving was done by Alfred Murdon.

[Sir Thomas Gresham's Exchange, from a Print in the Guildhall Library.]

The Charles Knight Collection

OLD LONDON

Landmarks Series – No. 3 Old Corn Exchange

The description of the activities of the Corn Exchange at this time are best portrayed through extracts from Charles Knight's London.

> "The number of establishments which are involved with supplying metropolis with corn and grain, seeds, malt, flour, meat and bread are as follows, according to the Post Office Directory for 1842:- Corn Merchants 75; Corn and Flour factors 138; Corn Dealers 243; millers 26; Bakers 1375; confectioners 285 ...
>
> ... The number of Corn vessels which do arrive is so great that warehouses, granaries and the river itself in many places, is completely blocked up; but the large quantity suddenly brought into the market depresses prices but duty mounts again ...
>
> When sold, the meter and his attendants are able to measure 600 or 700 quarters of oats a day and sometimes even 800. When wheat arrives in sacks it is measured at 70 an hour containing 35 quarters."

The Corn Markets in the City were numerous and many streets bear names connected with the corn, grain and associated trades such as baking – Cornhill, Bread Street, Basing Lane and of course Pudding Lane where the great fire of London (1666) started in a baker's shop. The main cornmarket was held at Cornhill but others were held at Newgate, Queenhithe and Southwark.

A Corn Exchange was established in 1747, being located in Mark Lane and it was extended to an adjoining building in 1828 and is the subject of this picture. Records of the Corn exchanges go back to the fifteenth century and show the traders to be very prosperous and often disliked because of their affluence. Externally the building consisted of an open colannade with Doric pillars 'very singularly spaced' with windows in the two upper stories. The interior formed the court in which the factors had their stands.

The artist of this picture was Henry Tiffin who exhibited his landscape drawings at the Royal Academy between 1845 and 1874 and the engraver was John Jackson.

[Corn Exchange, Mark Lane.]

The Charles Knight Collection

OLD LONDON

Landmarks Series – No. 4 Tower of London

The Tower has been prominent in English history as a fortress to a hateful place of horror and execution. Its Norman and medieval structure has been carefully maintained and it would seem that its state of preservation was equally well cared for at the time Charles Knight wrote his book about London. It is his observations that enable us to appreciate the terrors that the Tower has held for many unfortunate people.

> "The Tower seems to have had little horror for Sir Thomas More, unless indeed, it was from seeing its effect upon others. From his first entrance, when according to custom the porter demanded his uppermost garment as his fee, meaning, no doubt his cloak or some such similar valuable article – Sir Thomas, taking off his cap (with a latent consciousness that he would have no further need for it) said *that* was his uppermost garment, and he wished that it were of more value! On his final departure to the scaffold as he laid his head on the block, he remarked to the executioner – 'Prythee let me put my beard aside for that hath never committed treason.' The light hearted and high minded Chancellor still preserved all the delightful playfulness of manner which made him as much the beloved of his friends as his more important qualities made him the admiration of his contemporaries and of posterity."

Access to the Tower was frequently from the river and the scene in the picture shows Traitors Gate – the old water gate – through which many illustrious prisoners would have entered and seldom seen the light of day again.

The White Tower, the oldest part of the building was originally built by William the Conquerer to complete the fortifications of London at the eastern end of the Roman Wall. Yet the fortress has never been seriously assaulted and has been more a state prison and place of execution.

The picture was drawn by C. F. Sargeant and engraved by W. F. Green.

[The Tower. Time of Henry VI.]

The Charles Knight Collection

OLD LONDON

Landmarks Series – No. 5 The Customs House

The practice of levying taxes from the landing and embarkation of goods was first imposed by the Romans. In England the tax or toll was set by King Ethelred II (978 to 1016) for a duty to be charged on 'merchandise arriving at Billingsgate', which at that time appears to be the major landing place in London.

Charles Knight refers to the findings of John Stow, the renowned antiquarian and London historian, who noted in his 'Survey of London' which was published in 1598 that merchants and retailers not only profit for themselves and enrich the realm but also '... bear a good fleece which the Prince may shear when he seeth good.' Charles Knight adds to these comments:

> These exactions aided the sovereign in his necessities and induced him to encourage commerce of his subjects ... it was decided that every smaller boat should pay half a penny; a large boat with sails one penny; a keel (a ship we suppose) four pennies; a vessel with wood to give one piece of wood; a boat coming with fish to the bridge one half penny or one penny according to its size ...

During the middle ages penalties were enforced when landings were made and tolls not paid. The first Customs House was established in 1559 – the staff consisting of eight principal officers with up to six assistants and sixteen 'subordinates.'

The original Customs House was destroyed during the great fire of London in 1666 and the replacement building was also burnt out in 1718. A new building was erected within two years – it was 189 feet long and 29 feet wide – and its most striking feature was the Long Room in which all the general business took place. On 12 February 1814 the Customs House was yet again destroyed by fire. The new building was opened in 1817 and the Long Room (as in the inset) was even larger and grander than the previous building, its total dimensions being 190 feet in length, 66 feet wide rising to a height of 50 feet.

The splendid drawing (1841) is by Henry Anelay and the engraving by Alfred Slader.

[The Long Room, 1841.]

The Charles Knight Collection

OLD LONDON

Landmarks Series – No. 6 The General Post Office

> Of all the public departments under the direction and management of the State, the Post Office is at once the most popular and the most interesting in its operation and influence. It can scarcely any longer be regarded as an engine of taxation – its vast machinery being put into action almost solely for the advantage of the public ... millions of letters are now transmitted from one part of the earth to another – from kingdom to kingdom, from the metropolis to the most obscure hamlet, and from the latter to the antipodes.

This is the way Charles Knight describes the value of the postal service which he defines as a 'very ancient institution' having been set up mainly to communicate between the various departments of state and their agencies in the provinces. In 1635 a proclamation was issued 'for settling of the letter office of England and Scotland' which was the first attempt to put the Post Office on a 'modern footing'. In 1649 there was a dispute by which the City of London set up its own private system but the Commons passed a resolution asserting their exclusive right to control of such establishments. Nevertheless private companies survived because they carried mail at much cheaper rates but the passing of an Act in 1656 fully established the authority of the Government posts. Let Charles Knight explain the scene.

> The service was very inefficiently performed and the rate of travelling did not exceed four miles per hour. Time Bills are headed 'Haste, Haste, Post Haste!' The mails were conveyed on horse back or in a cart ... and even now over fifty years after and on the great roads, five miles an hour was considered as quite 'going ahead'.
>
> The era of Mail Coaches embraces about half a century (1790-1840). Their origin, maturity, perfection and gradual displacement by the railways all took place within this short period. In 1836 there were 54 four horse mails in England, 30 in Ireland and 10 in Scotland. The English mail coach was strongly characteristic of the national energy and spirit, and also of the natural taste.

The main Post Office building in this picture was started in May 1824 and completed in September 1829 – its dimensions being 389 feet long, 130 feet wide and 64 feet high; the size of which was justified by the increase in volume of postal traffic following the introduction of the Penny Post in 1840 which was set up by Rowland Hill. The artist was Henry Tiffin and the engraving was by John Jackson.

[Hall of the Post Office, 1841.]

Waterways

1. OLD LONDON BRIDGE
2. THAMES TUNNEL
3. OLD BLACKFRIARS BRIDGE
4. EAST INDIA DOCK
5. ST. JAMES'S PARK
6. THAMES CORN BARGE

The Charles Knight Collection

OLD LONDON

Waterways Series – No. 1 Old London Bridge

'London Bridge is falling down' is not a fallacy. From the first wooden bridge built across the Thames until quite recent times the bridge has been destroyed or damaged by floods, fire or battles on numerous occasions. The first stone bridge was built by Peter of Colechurch in 1176 and finally completed in 1209. It was 926 feet long and a 20 feet wide passageway and 40 feet width between the full extent of the parapets. The highest point between the river and the bridge was 60 feet and had 20 arches and various piers. It also contained water wheels to produce power and operate the corn mill. Locks and many other buildings were also erected of which the most acclaimed was the Chapel.

The description by Charles Knight tells the story:

> Around 1280 mention is made of "innumerable people dwelling on the bridge" and as this was only some 70 years after it had been finished, it seems probable that there were some houses upon from the first ... other erections were undertaken the most famous of which was the Chapel dedicated to St. Thomas a Becket which stood on the east side above the tenth or central pier ... 30 feet in length, it had four buttresses crowned with crocketed spires.
>
> Although London Bridge remained substantially what its first architect made it till it was taken down – there was no part of it, not excepting even the arches and the piers themselves that had not been modified or transformed in the long interval between 1205 and 1832.

London records show that by 1358 there were 138 shops on the bridge above which were three and sometimes four storey houses. Its more sinister connections are with the Tower of London. Heads of unfortunates were piked and left at the end of London Bridge. These can be seen in the picture.

The engraving in this reproduction was drawn in 1841 by Harden Melville and thought to be from an original sketch by John Norden drawn around 1615 and Visscher's Prospect of London. The engraver was Rembault.

The bridge as depicted in the engraving was finally demolished in 1832, the houses and shops having been removed between 1758 and 1762. John Rennie and his son of the same name designed and built a new London Bridge which was opened in 1831 (inset) and it was this bridge that was transported stone by stone to the United States of America and was rebuilt at Lake Havasu City, Arizona.

London Bridge in 1827.

The Charles Knight Collection

OLD LONDON

Waterways Series – No. 2 Thames Tunnel

The first tunnel under the Thames was eventually completed and opened in 1843 and was the first major underwater thoroughfare in the world. It was started in the autumn of 1807 but preparation and surveying had been poor and after tunnelling through 300 metres and encountering three collapses of the roof the project was abandoned in January 1808.

In 1825 the brilliant French engineer Marc Brunel came up with a plan to build the tunnel using a new tunnelling shield and machine that he had patented in 1818. There were many problems and tragedies as the difficult and dangerous task progressed but the ingenuity and resolution of Marc Brunel and his son prevailed and the task was completed. Charles Knight describes the scene:

> The excavators now commenced their work, cutting away the ground which was raised to the top of the shaft by a steam engine, there placed, and which also relieved them of the water which often impended their descent ... at the first construction of the shaft, it seemed to our eyes, not initiated in the wonders of engineering, not one of the least marvels of this altogether marvellous work.

On 25 March 1843 the tunnel between Wapping and Rotherhithe was opened to the public but due to a restricted budget was only used by pedestrians and horse drawn carts. The entrance and stairway was extremely attractive and seats were provided at intervals so that travellers could rest during their journey under the Thames.

Its dimensions of each of its two passageways were 1300 feet long, 15 feet 4 inches high and 16 feet 3 inches wide. Total cost of building the tunnel was £454,714 and the one penny toll on pedestrians made it impossible for the original outlay to be recovered. The tunnel was sold to the London and Brighton Railway Company in 1865 and later became part of the London Underground system forming the East London line.

The artist of this very fine drawing (1843) was Thomas Shepherd who was renowned for his drawings of London which were '... outstanding for this skill and beauty.' The engraver was M. Murdon.

[Longitudinal Section of the Tunnel, showing the Shield and the mode of working it.]

The Charles Knight Collection

OLD LONDON

Waterways Series – No. 3 Old Blackfriars Bridge

An increasing need for more bridges across the lower reaches of the Thames to link north and south London led to a government competition in 1759 to decide the best design. The winner was Robert Mylne, a young Scot, and the majestic bridge as depicted in this engraving was the result. It was opened amongst much controversy on 19 November 1769 due to the imposition of a halfpenny toll on weekdays and one penny at the weekends. It was the third bridge to span the Thames in central London and was originally called Pitt's Bridge.

Charles Knight reflects on how decisions came to be made regarding the building of Blackfriars Bridge:

> Maitland insisted on the importance for the City of London 'to seriously reflect on these schemes ... which now (1756) little more than embryos must be speedily acted upon.' The spot chosen was a memorable one in history, but the connection of things now it is in constant use are strangely contrasted between monasteries and friars, bridges, omnibuses and cabs.
>
> Among the buildings removed there are two that must not pass without notice. Ludgate, the once famous gate to the City first built by the Barons of King John was sold for just £148 – the presumed value of no more than the materials. The other building destroyed in the building process was the most beautiful bridge erected across the Fleet Ditch by Sir George Waterman in 1672.

Blackfriars derives its name from the 13th century monastery which was established close to the river by the Dominican Monks who were known as the 'Black Friars'. This is the point where the Fleet river ran into the Thames but all that remains today is a pipe way. Close to the north end of the bridge was the site of the first covered theatre in London, built in 1596, where it is thought that William Shakespeare acted. The spot is known as 'Playhouse Yard'.

The bridge was altered and strengthened many times. This drawing is of the renovated structure as it appeared in 1842. Although of beautiful architectural appearance it could not cope with the increasingly heavy traffic, and was demolished in 1860. It was replaced by the existing bridge which was designed by Joseph Cubitt and opened by Queen Victoria in 1869.

The artist of this fine perspective drawing was Henry Tiffin, the landscape painter. The engraver was John Jackson.

[Old Blackfriars Bridge, 1836.]

J. JACKSON

The Charles Knight Collection

OLD LONDON

Waterways Series – No. 4 East India Dock

At the time Charles Knight was writing and editing his History of London, British trade and industry was at a peak. London was the trading centre of the world as a result of the Industrial Revolution and the fast expanding Empire, consequently exporting heavy machinery and other goods and importing a variety of merchandise from other lands throughout the World.

The East India Docks was located at Blackwall and were under the same ownership as the West India Docks – both docks covering 295 acres. The water depth of the basins was never less than 23 feet. Around 1840 an analysis of dock storage shows that contained 180,000 tons of merchandise valued at over £20 million including "148,563 casks of sugar, 70,875 barrels and 433,668 bags of coffee, 35,158 pipes of rum and madeira, 14000 logs of mahogany, 21000 tons of logwood besides other articles."

Charles Knight observes:

> "Again steam navigation was relatively unimportant but a short time ago, that it is scarcely a matter of surprise that none of the Docks are calculated for steamers of the largest class without the paddle-wheels being taken off; and yet vessels of this description are gradually obtaining possession of trade formerly employing sailing vessels of comparatively small burthen ... one of the objections to the accommodation of these steam-vessels in the docks is the risk of fire."

Security at the docks was very severe and the work tasks rigorous. It was often the practice to discharge crews as soon as a ship entered port but after 1840 crews were allowed to stay on board subject to strict regulations regarding the use of fires. The docks mainly dealt with wholesalers in the City and small lighters would transport goods upstream. The East India Dock Road and the Commercial Road were made for this purpose and cartage by 'cart or wagon' from Blackwall to the City was 5 shillings per ton.

The artist of this drawing was J. Jarvis and the engraver was F. Smyth.

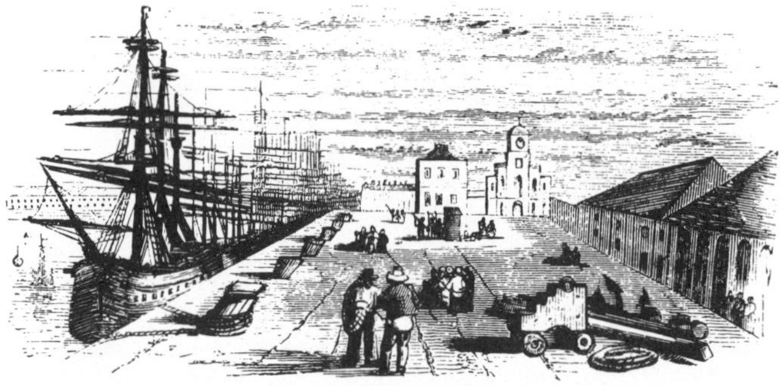

[East India Import Dock.]

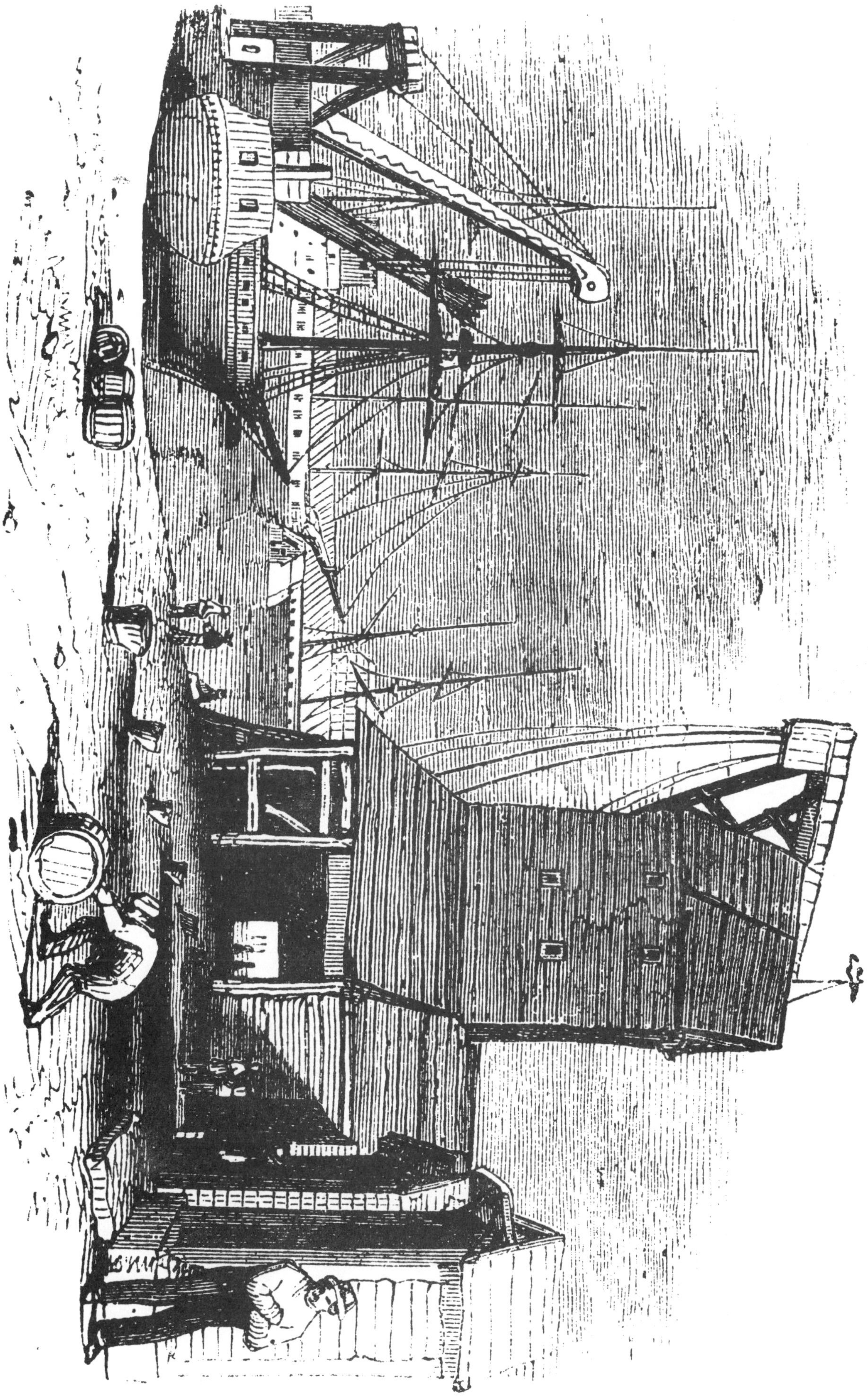

The Charles Knight Collection

OLD LONDON

Waterways Series – No. 5 St. James's Park

St. James's Park is the oldest and smallest of all the London Metropolitan parks and according to Charles Knight 'certainly the prettiest'. Up to the reign of Henry VIII it was like many other parts of London being very wet and marshy. In 1532 he built a passage and massive gateway leading from Whitehall Palace into the Park, drained the marsh and enclosed it.

James I decided that silk could be produced in St. James's Park and in 1608 many thousands of Mulberry trees were imported from France. In 1629 a grant was authorized for '... the custody of the garden, mulberry trees and silk worms near St. James in the County of Middlesex.' The silk worms eventually disappeared and what was the Mulberry Garden was later enclosed into Buckingham House later to be the Palace. Charles the Second made improvements but it was still only used as a deer nursery, duck pond, Tilt yard and sporting area on the Pall Mall side.

It was not until 1828 that Nash was commissioned to convert the Park from a 'formal swampy meadow' into a beautiful luxuriant looking garden. The Park took its name from being connected with the palace of St. James's which Henry VIII built on the site of St. James's Hospital.

Charles Knight describes an early Summer evening in 1838:

> Those who have dined in the fashionable West End enjoy themselves in the rays of the already setting sun. Hundreds are walking amongst the shrubbery, seated on chairs by the waterside or amusing themselves with the water fowl ...

The locality around St. James's Palace and Park was famous in the 18th century for its Chocolate and Coffee houses which were the forerunners of today's traditional London Clubs. Specialist shops were set up to service the Royal Households many of which still remain. St. James's Palace is the official residence of HRH The Prince of Wales.

Thomas Shepherd was the artist of this drawing and F. Smyth was the engraver.

[Rosamond's Pond.—1758.]

The Charles Knight Collection

OLD LONDON

Waterways Series – No. 6 Thames Corn Barge

Prior to the escalation of bridges and tunnels traversing the Thames the prime mode of transport between the Docks and the city or from ship to shore was by the use of various types of barge, lighter and ferry. The Thames Corn Barges were of a broad beam construction to enable them to carry as many sacks of grain as possible. They were also used by the 'meters' who controlled the measuring and collecting of taxes. Farmers from Kent and Essex would bring their grain to London in sacks and these would be weighed and secured before being transferred to the Thames Corn Barges for loading onto the Ocean going ships.

Charles Knight explains:

> On arrival a cargo of corn or grain is subjected to a variety of regulations ... a number of dues are collected by the City Authorities for water baillage, groundage, Lord Mayor's and crocket dues before the goods were put into the docks huge warehouses ... 'Corn meters' who control receipt, despatch and loading procedures are appointed by a committee of the Corporation called the Coal and Corn Committee and control the activities of the 150 'corn meters' ... sometimes they have to accompany small corn barges to any part of the river between Staines and Yantlet Creek.
>
> When the ship is ready for delivery, the meter and seven or sometimes eight of the fellowship porters go aboard. Two of the latter dip into the bulk with their concave wooden shovels and the meter completes the filling up of the bushels, then one of the two porters passes the strike over the surface and the third holds the sack into which the other two pour the contents of the bushel ... this is then hoisted up by the three porters on the deck, one of whom bears it over the ship's side.

The artist of this picture was Arthur Mead and the engraver was George Hollaway.

[St. Katherine's Docks.]

Streets & Suburbs

1. ISLINGTON GREEN
2. KNIGHTSBRIDGE – ONE MILE FROM LONDON
3. ELEPHANT AND CASTLE ALMSHOUSES
4. SEVEN DIALS
5. ST. JOHN'S GATE CLERKENWELL
6. WARWICK LANE

The Charles Knight Collection

OLD LONDON

Streets and Suburbs Series – No. 1 Islington Green

By the middle of the nineteenth century the country byways of London were beginning to become heavily used by Hackney and Stage coaches, horse trams and trucks. The age of steam had arrived and railways began to snake their way out to the London suburbs. The population of London rose from around one million at the time of this drawing to seven million by the end of the nineteenth century. The countryside once only a mile or so from the city suddenly became ten miles away.

Charles Knight refers to a number of 'palacial buildings' in Islington and he describes a journey where he … 'reached Islington Green occasioning to stop and gaze on the suburban gentility of Hollaway and admire the architectural grandeur of Highbury …'

Originating from the true British name of 'Iseldon' it appeared in the Domesday Book as '… 1000 acres of arable land alone'. The name was conjectured to signify the Lower Fort which was linked to the Roman Camp at Highbury located close to the main Roman road of Ermine Street.

Islington was a health and pleasure spot for Londoners having, it was said, health giving waters from the wells in the area, one of which was the famous Sadlers Wells. Its theatre once managed by the famous clown Joseph Grimaldi is close by. The suburb was renowned for its Coffee Houses and entertainment. At the north end of the Green stood the famous Collins Music Hall of Marie Lloyd fame and it is not far from this point where, the reformist and radical, Thomas Paine laid the groundwork for the American Constitution.

Islington was also well known for its Inns and Public Houses which included 'The Pied Bull' the favourite haunt of Sir Walter Raleigh, 'The Highway Barn' recalling the original country setting and the galleried inn of 'The Angel'. The nearby Spa Fields was the location of the ancient Gooseberry Fair.

This engraving of Islington Green drawn in 1841 by J. S. Flint and prepared for print by one of Charles Knight's most favoured engravers, S. Sly, gives us a glimpse of London's suburbia just before the massive growth of London occurred. The map below is related to a population return of 1831 indicating that within the eight mile radius from St. Pauls there was a population of 1,776,000 inhabitants. Charles Knight points out that at the time of writing his book, in 1841, the same number of people lived within four miles of St. Pauls.

[Eight Miles round St. Paul's.]

S.SLY.

The Charles Knight Collection

OLD LONDON

Streets and Suburbs Series – No. 2 Knightsbridge One Mile from London

The area of Knightsbridge, Hyde Park and Kensington developed as an elite part of London, being close to the royal palaces and consequently enhanced. William III and Queen Anne acquired various sections of which the Official grant deed describes as:

> '... all that ditch and fence which divide Hyde Park from the other lands and possessions of the said Park ... wood, underwood and timber trees growing and being within, upon or about ... beginning from the south highway leading to the top of Kensington, and from thence crossing to the north highway leading to the town of Acton, which said piece of ground is by this grant disparked forever.'

The roads and highways from the South and West of England converged upon Knightsbridge and Hyde Park Corner and according to Charles Knight travellers could become somewhat confused:

> The suburbs of London continued to be full of puzzling inscriptions down to a recent date. The system of measuring the roads out of London by some well known centrical object, such as the Standard in Cornhill (a conduit once known to every passenger), was a right system, and ought to have been a uniform one. But the other system was that of measuring the roads from some point where London was supposed to terminate ... so Hyde Park Corner has also become obsolete; but it was a real barrier point to London when its great gates stretched across the road, with its wondrous illumination of a dozen oil lamps before the days of gas.
>
> The managers of this road have now begun, as they conceive, to reform the milestones; and these dumb oracles tell us that we are "One Mile from London" or "Two Miles from London". What is London? Where does it begin? Where does it end? Is not the character of London always shifting? We now call Tottenham Court Road, London; but it was not London a century ago.
>
> Knightsbridge is now as much London as Tottenham Court Road. In London, then, a stranger is told he is a mile from London. This of course is unintelligible.

The artist of this drawing is Henry Anelay who exhibited his landscapes at the Royal Academy for over 20 years. The engraver is P. Andrew who was employed by Charles Knight to help illustrate the 'Penny Magazines'.

[The Serpentine.]

The Charles Knight Collection

OLD LONDON

Streets and Suburbs Series – No. 3 Elephant and Castle Almshouses

The Elephant and Castle was one of the many hostelries on the main highway from London to the southern ports of Southampton and Portsmouth. It was another of those many places that was said to be 'One Mile from Cornhill Standard'.

From London Bridge the road meandered through the badly lit streets of Borough where robbers lurked at every turn. This was the murky side of London as portrayed by Charles Dickens who was writing his novels around the same time as Charles Knight was attempting to educate the illiterate 'masses'.

The whole area comes within Southwark which can be termed as the first suburb of London being linked to the City by London Bridge. Despite its apparent poverty it was nevertheless an area of considerable interest as Charles Knight explains:

> If one were suddenly asked to point out that portion of the Metropolis which more than any other is crowded with the most deeply interesting associations, the Borough would hardly we think be the chosen place.
>
> The very name seems to repel all ideas of a romantic or poetical nature. Yet if there be classic ground in London, it is this. Standing upon the foot of that bridge which has replaced the venerable piece of antiquity so connected with the local history of Southwark – what a host of recollections of some of the mightiest intellects are connected with localities comprised of half a circle just a few hundred yards from the river!
>
> In the street now known as Clink Street was Shakespeare's London residence as late as 1609. 'The Tabard' of Chaucer yet lies unnoticed before us and there are few more ancient streets than that in which the famous hostelry is situated – the High Street of Southwark. Others of fame – the Boar's Head, Mermaid and the Talbot all are in this street.

Among the other places close by was the sight of the famous Globe Theatre where Shakespeare acted and which he partly owned. 'The Globe' was built in 1599 and demolished in 1644 as a result of the Puritans purge on theatrical performances.

The almshouses at the 'Elephant' were probably the best location in the area for living. They were built by the church to house 'the elderly'. The subject is finely portrayed by the accomplished landscape artist Henry Anelay who was also one of the principal artists used by the Illustrated London News between 1843 and 1855. The engraver was T. Heaviside.

[The Talbot, 1841.]

The Charles Knight Collection

OLD LONDON

Streets and Suburbs Series – No. 4 Seven Dials

The area of St. Giles and the converging routes leading to Seven Dials was one of the many areas of London which was originally established as a place for the affluent traders by the early eighteenth century as Charles Knight expresses it '... was a place of retreat for noisome and squalid outcasts.' Charles II attempted to make the area more respectable but it was soon taken over by '... the power of counter agents whose careers were associated with haggardry and hostility to the law which became as bad as its close neighbours in the Rookery.'

This was the evidence of squalor which appalled Charles Knight and he was outspoken about it both in the written words of his 'Penny Magazines' which he originated for the 'Society for the Diffusion of Useful Knowledge' in 1831 and his vocal complaints to various influential people. It is probable that Charles Dickens was influenced by the publications of Knight as he first started writing about the depravity of the poor around 1835 when Dicken's first published his 'Street Sketches' and 'Sketches of London' in the Morning Chronicle.

The streets around central London were 'narrow and irregular, unlit in most instances and totally unprotected by any form of policing except perhaps in the vicinity of the more affuent classes.' Charles Knight explains further:

> The whole area of Soho, Clare Market, Seven Dials and others offered facilities for unforeseen attacks and for the escape of malefactors. The straggling character of the suburban villages and numerous fields that intervened between the inhabited spots also afforded many lurking places.
>
> The civil authorities nor the 'Watchmen' made any attempt to check the rude, hardened attitude of the vagrants nor to regulate scavenging, accidents and violence in the streets and clear the filth and nuisances that are still in London.
>
> But it was all related to the plight of the destitute and unemployed who are not only uncertain where they are to lay themselves at night but where the food, if any, to satisfy their first cravings of hunger in the cold or wet morning may be found.

The extent of the squalid dwellings set so close to the affluence of 'high society' London increased rapidly. By the time of Charles Knight's death in 1873 the population, mainly consisting of poorly paid 'working class' people, was six times what it had been in 1831. It was they who had no alternative but to live in slums such as Seven Dials.

The artist of this picture was Henry Tiffin and the engraver was John Jackson.

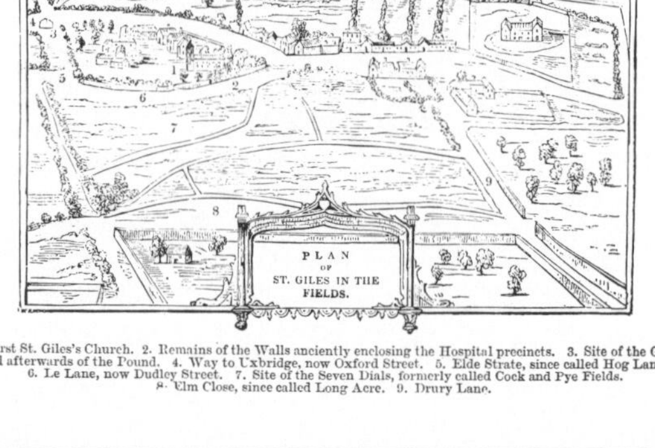

1. The first St. Giles's Church. 2. Remains of the Walls anciently enclosing the Hospital precincts. 3. Site of the Gallows, and afterwards of the Pound. 4. Way to Uxbridge, now Oxford Street. 5. Elde Strate, since called Hog Lane. 6. Le Lane, now Dudley Street. 7. Site of the Seven Dials, formerly called Cock and Pye Fields. 8. Elm Close, since called Long Acre. 9. Drury Lane.

ESTABLISHMENT.

The Charles Knight Collection

OLD LONDON

Streets and Suburbs Series – No. 5 St. John's Gate Clerkenwell

There is nothing more descriptive of the scene of expanding London and in particular of Clerkenwell than Charles Knight's own words:

> Those who reside on the outskirts of London a variety of changes to a very marked degree. North, South, East and West – on all sides – a period of twenty years is sufficient to change the whole appearance of the border of London, if such a border can be found. The parish of Clerkenwell was just such a border two centuries ago for it was separated very decidedly from the village of Islington – green fields and country paths forming the connection from one to the other. But now where are the green fields and the paths?
>
> When passing through the little avenue called 'Jerusalem Passage' which leads from St. John's Square to Clerkenwell Green we have on the left a mass of houses which occupy both sides of the site of the Priory wall. Imagine Clerkenwell Green to be really green, bounded on the south by a wall and a postern gate through which the priors and monks had access and egress ... and the north wall a Nunnery also with a postern gate. Imagine also a fine open country on all sides (except perhaps the south) with vineyards and meadows, and springs and rivulets. We shall then have an idea of what this spot once was.

St. John's Gate was erected in 1504 and was originally the south gate of a once wealthy Priory of the order of St. John of Jerusalem which was founded around 1130. Clerkenwell originally derived its name from 'the clerk's well' but in the seventeenth century its value as a supplier of water diminished and on the arrival of the French Huguenots Clerkenwell became a centre connected with Jewellers, clockmakers and opticians. In consequence fine residences were established but in the massive growth of population the deterioration which distressed Charles Knight occurred and slum housing took over. Clerkenwell Green was the centre of political activity during the times of the Chartist movement in the 1840's.

The artist of this picture was Thomas Shepherd whose drawings of London were highly acclaimed for their skill and beauty. The engraver was Stephen Sears.

[St. John's Hospital: from Hollar.]

OLD JERUSALEM

The Charles Knight Collection

OLD LONDON

Streets and Suburbs Series – No. 6 Warwick Lane

The splendid College building in the narrow cobbled street of Warwick Lane was the home of the Society of Physicians for over 150 years. The original college set up under a charter in 1522 established a meeting place in Knight Rider Street but moved to a permanent location at Amen Corner a few years later. The Great Fire of London in 1666 completely destroyed these buildings and in 1669 a piece of ground was purchased in Warwick Lane and a design commissioned from Sir Christopher Wren.

The building was superb in proportion and style and was recognised as one of the most important of its kind in the City. Sadly by the time this picture was drawn it had delapidated considerably from its former glory, being used as a meat storage house and workshops – the Society having moved to more modern buildings at Pall Mall East. But Charles Knight's account enables us to envisage its former glories.

> Its great size and noble proportions were in every way worthy of its illustrious architect. The shape and character of the building was consistent throughout; the porch was octangular with eight windows on eight exterior faces and a lantern over the dome. The entrance hall was sixty feet from floor to ceiling with a truly magnificent staircase ran upwards through it with elaborately carved balusters and an elegantly decorated ceiling. There were other fine features throughout – fine oak wood carving, rich marble, elaborate stucco ornaments – a truly magnificent building inside and out.

The Society of Physicians who had occupied the glorious building for so many years had a strange history before any of their colleges were established. People providing medical help in the middle ages were of ten labelled as sorcerers and using the magic of astrology and '... the powers of the supernatural to drive out demons' were frequently ridiculed and imprisoned. It was Henry VIII's Act of Parliament in 1511 which eventually led to the formation of the College and the granting of 'letters patent' to the Society.

Thomas Shepherd was the artist of this drawing and was recognised as one of the finest illustrators of London Buildings between 1817 and 1842. The engraver was Alfred Slader.

[Royal College of Physicians, Pall Mall East.]

PAIN
MEAT COMMISSION SALESMAN
TYLORS
BELL INN

The Penny Magazine

The Charles Knight Collection

OLD LONDON

The Penny Magazine of the Society for the Diffusion of Useful Knowledge

The Penny Magazine was the publication which gave Charles Knight his widest recognition by the ever increasing English population. As we have seen the weekly journal gained enormous acclaim and popularity and Knight was extremely and rightly proud of his achievement. He wrote an editorial in 1835 in which he said:

> Our facts have supplied the materials for exciting the curiosity of a million readers. This consideration furnishes the most convincing answer to those (if any there now remain) who assert that General Education is an evil.

It seems fitting in many respects that we should come almost to the end of this book with the inclusion of a complete copy of one of Charles Knight's Penny Magazines plus a monthly supplement which was a regular feature of the journal. Today the content is equally as fascinating and instructive as it was 150 years ago but it also enables us to see how Charles Knight saw Old England and Europe.

Throughout this book we have concentrated on Charles Knight's LONDON and we will continue to extend our series of drawings and designs relating to the Metropolis. But in Charles Knight's Old England lies another wonderful vision of our Country as it was in the early Victorian period. Following on the theme of the works published by Knight we will produce another series to recognise the genius of a great writer, publisher and his supporting artists. The contents therefore of the PENNY MAGAZINE for July 29, 1837 provides us not only with a further glimpse of Old London but also the treasured Lake District of 'the wonderful North Country.'

The Penny Magazine was started in 1832 and as we have seen was immensely successful for a considerable period. Around 1842 it became more specialized concentrating on long series related to nature, literature and art and as a result lost its original popularity. It ceased publication in 1845 but in the intervening years had provided many with wonderful entertainment whilst at the same time helping to educate the populous.

There is no doubt that it was Charles Knight who not only originated the name 'Penny Magazine' in his capacity as publisher but was also the originator of the name taken up by the 'Society for the Diffusion of Useful Knowledge'. Lord Brougham had attempted to form a similar society in 1825 and had named it the 'Society for Promoting General Knowledge.' However Charles Knight put forward his proposed title to Lord Brougham and this was accepted.

The objects of the new society were much in tune with Knight's own thinking. It would seem that he had sought out leading figures from the radical reformists who could sponsor such a group and it would appear that much of the credit for the formation and success of SPUK should go to Charles Knight. Its objectives were defined as '...the imparting of useful information to all classes of the community, particularly to such as are unable to avail themselves of experienced teachers, or may prefer learning by themselves.' The committee consisted of '...not less than 40 and not more than 60 members' and these included many influential people such as Lord John Russell, Lord Althorp, Dr Arnold of Rugby and Rowland Hill of 'Penny Post' fame.

The Society published a wide range of publications in addition to the Penny Magazine. These included British Almanac, Working Man's Almanac, Library of Entertaining Knowledge, Gallery of Portraits and Maps. The Penny Cyclopedia became so complex and expensive that it caused the society to cease activities in 1845.

THE

PENNY MAGAZINE

OF

THE SOCIETY

FOR THE

DIFFUSION OF USEFUL KNOWLEDGE.

1837.

LONDON
CHARLES KNIGHT & CO., 22, LUDGATE STREET.

Price 6s. in Twelve Monthly Parts, and 7s. 6d. bound in Cloth.

THE PENNY MAGAZINE

OF THE

Society for the Diffusion of Useful Knowledge.

341.] PUBLISHED EVERY SATURDAY. [JULY 29, 1837.

A LOOKING-GLASS FOR LONDON.—No. XIX.

TRADE—REGENT STREET, AND THE SHOPS OF THE "WEST END."

[Regent Street, looking North, from the Quadrant.]

THE "east end" of London knows little or nothing of those elegant modern refinements in shopkeeping which, under the names of bazaars and arcades, are familiar to the "west end," and to various provincial towns. The shopkeepers of the city, though many of them are bestowing much of splendid decoration on their premises, still act on the maxim that a shop is neither more nor less than a shop, a place for positive buying and selling, and not intended to accommodate a congregation of loungers. Bazaars and arcades are, therefore, more intended for those who have time and money at their disposal, and are, occasionally, uncertain how to spend either, than for the sober, specific, earnest purposes of trade. Thus, what is sold in these places belongs principally to the lighter and more elegant branches of traffic: the pastry-cook may show himself amongst the sellers, but the baker and the butcher would be out of their element. In the shops of the arcade, and on the tables and counters of the bazaar, are spread out whatever is thought likely to attract the eye, and tempt to purchase. Hither comes the jeweller, with his rings, and chains, and seals, and watches; the perfumer has his oils, and combs, and brushes; the toyman with his dancing-jacks, and ever-galloping horsemen, tiny trumpets, drums, and violins, Chinese puzzles, and musical boxes; the tobacconist offers his cigars and scented snuffs; the stationer and the music-seller exhibit prints, music, and musical instruments; while the shoemaker, milliner, and bonnet-maker display the neatest proofs of their respective handicrafts.

The first arcade we meet with in proceeding westward is the Lowther Arcade, which runs from the Strand to Adelaide Street, at the back of St. Martin's church. This is a fine passage, lofty and spacious, and lighted by ornamented circular skylights. The Burlington Arcade, in Piccadilly, is narrower but much longer than the Lowther Arcade. It is favourably situated near the thoroughfares of the west end, and is itself a considerable thoroughfare. In Pimlico, where, about ten years ago, were fields, now occupied by the fine houses which constitute Belgrave Square, Wilton Crescent, &c., there is the Pantechnicon—a spirited attempt to combine on one spot all the supplies requisite for a rich and fashionable population. The Pantechnicon is a compound of the arcade and the bazaar, and aims at a higher and more solid character than either have yet made for themselves. It consists of two large and distinct buildings—one termed the "carriage department," devoted to the purposes its name indicates; the other, having two paved passages or arcades, with shops on either side, stairs leading to show-rooms above, and wine-vaults below, while a significant "☞ To the Bazaar" intimates that lighter and more elegant trifles are not forgotten in the attention paid to carriages, furniture, and household supplies.

There are various bazaars at the west end, of which

the more remarkable are, the one in Soho Square, the first started in London, another in Baker Street, Portman Square, and a third in the building in Oxford Street, which occupies the site of what was termed the Pantheon. The Pantheon was a handsome building devoted to purposes of amusement; it was nearly all burned in 1792; and the present building, which retains the portico of the former one, has, after some vicissitudes, been devoted to the purposes of a bazaar. The ground-floor is neatly set round with tables, after the manner of a "fancy fair;" a flight of stairs leads to the upper floor, which is partly occupied in the same way; and a number of other rooms are set apart as a picture gallery, where pictures are hung up for sale. An open space in the centre of the upper floor, which is railed round, permits the light to fall from the roof on the lower floor, and from hence the visiter can look down on the not uninteresting scene below. In the rear of the building is a conservatory, where plants and flowers are exhibited for sale, and which contains a mimic fountain and basin with gold and silver fish.

Regent Street is divided into two distinct portions or streets. The first street, which is the shortest, runs up from Pall Mall to Piccadilly, terminating in an open circular space, called the Circus. The Haymarket on one side, and St. James's Street at some little distance on the other, run parallel with this Regent Street, all three extending from Pall Mall to Piccadilly. The view from the Circus down Regent Street, which slopes towards St. James's Park, is excellent. The street, though rather short, is broad and spacious: the view extends across Pall Mall, to the steps leading into the park, on the top of which is the pillar erected to the memory of the Duke of York. From the Circus we turn round, through the colonnaded curve called the Quadrant, into the upper portion of Regent Street. The Quadrant is certainly a singular street. Its form is a curve: colonnades supported on iron pillars run along on either side, underneath which the foot passengers walk, and the shops here are of a similar character to the shops of an arcade. In cold, moist, wintry weather, these colonnades are dark, heavy-looking, and cheerless, even though they afford a shelter from the rain, while the sombre aspect of gas-lit shops in mid-day adds to the dreariness. In summer they are pleasant, cool and shady, but still are lacking in that peculiar kind of effect which we associate with a colonnade in sultry weather. A calm, bright, moonlit night, is the best time for viewing with advantage a style of building which can hardly be said to be adapted to the character of our climate.

On emerging from the Quadrant, the upper Regent Street is spread before us; and if the period be the busy "season," and the time of day from one or two o'clock till four or five, or even six, with a bright summer sun pouring its radiance over spacious street and dingy alley, the view is, of its kind, one of the finest in the world. The newest fashions are displayed on the street; rows of carriages are drawn up at the edge of each pavement; loungers on foot, or on horseback, or whirling their cabriolets along, pass up and down; at the doors of many of the shops forms are ostentatiously placed by the considerate shopmen, on which footmen recline, in liveries of various hues, awaiting the pleasure of their masters or mistresses within; shopmen, trimly dressed, step out to receive the commands of those who do not choose to alight from their carriages, or else to deliver the purchases with a polite and humble attention; and now and then, a hackney-coach, or a cab, or an omnibus with its dozen passengers at sixpence each, or a poor beggar on the pavement, make their appearance, as if to illustrate by the force of contrast all this showy splendour. What an amount of wealth does this single street indicate!

Bond Street, divided into Old and New, is a short distance from Regent Street, running parallel with it from Piccadilly to Oxford Street. It is still a much-frequented place, and many of its shops are elegant and grand, though its old consequence as a fashionable lounging-street has been somewhat eclipsed by its more magnificent-looking rival.

The long line of Oxford Street is full of many and remarkable contrasts. Shops of every character are to be found in it; the baker and the confectioner, with their open windows, and smoking buns, and tarts that the sun has changed in colour; the fishmonger drenching his shop with water, to preserve his stock from the effects of the heat; the public-house, at the doors of which stable-boys, footmen, and working men may be seen entering or emerging; the coffee-shop; the trunk-maker; the hosier, in a little shop where there seems hardly room to turn between the shelves and the counter; the saloon-like place where the mercer unrolls his silks; the little stalls on the edge of the pavement, loaded with cabbage and cauliflowers, green pease, and new potatoes. The best part of Oxford Street is from a little east of Regent Street, proceeding westwards. Being a great thoroughfare, it is perpetually thronged; carriages, stage-coaches, cabriolets, and omnibuses are ever rolling past—for Oxford Street is the Cheapside of the "west end."

We have already alluded, on former occasions, to the other streets of the west-end, which are noted places—such as Pall-Mall and St. James's Street. The great thoroughfares, or promenades, are Pall-Mall, St. James's Street, Piccadilly, New and Old Bond Streets, Albemarle Street, the two Regent Streets, Oxford Street, with the arcades and bazaars. There are many fine shops here and there, some of them in very quiet-looking places, scattered amongst the private houses in the different streets. Charing Cross, the west end of the Strand, and part of Whitehall Street may be added to the remarkable or noted streets.

In speaking of the "west end," and associating with it the idea of grandeur and fashion, we must not forget that there are numerous streets, insinuated, as it were, into the crevices of those spacious and magnificent streets, which proclaim that the rich and noble do not occupy exclusively this large division of London. For where else could the working population be sheltered, whose business it is to wait upon and supply the demands of their wealthier neighbours? From the magnificence of Portland Place we can pass in a few minutes into little streets and courts, some of them dirty and disagreeable-looking; and, after wandering amid the noble mansions that occupy the streets on the east side of Hyde Park, we can cross Bond Street and Regent Street, and arrive in places where it is to be feared that much of ignorance and much of vice are still to be found. The least instructed and least reflecting portion of the community have a tendency to settle down by the side of the rich, and, by contributing to their conveniences, earn a livelihood. It is this very class, however, who are least capable of resisting evil example, or of denying themselves an excessive indulgment of their appetites—and it is to be feared that there is, comparatively, more of vice amongst the under classes of the west than of the east end of London.

LINDISFARN, OR HOLY ISLAND.

THOSE portions of the County Palatine of Durham which are known as North Durham, and which lie on the north side of the River Tyne, are divided into Bedlingtonshire, Norhamshire, and Islandshire. The two latter are contiguous upon the southern bank of the Tweed, and the former consists of a district upon the southern coast of Northumberland. The so-called shires of Norham and Island are coextensive with parishes bearing the same names, and may be considered as the most ancient possessions of the see of Durham. The parish of Island, or Holy Island, in its southern extremity, extends to that part of the right bank of the Tweed where it falls into the sea at Berwick, and reaches on the east from the sea again to the Tweed on the north: it is divided into the five chapelries of Holy Island, the mother-church, Kyloe, Lowick, Ancroft, and Tweedmouth. This parish derives its historical importance as containing the island from which Christianity first shed her benignant rays on Northumberland; and which for four centuries was not only the episcopal residence of the see which is now known as the bishopric of Durham, but the repository of learning in the North of England. This island the ancient Britons called *Inis Medicante*, but its familiar appellation was *Lindisfarn*, until the sanctity of its inhabitants procured for it the name of *Helichlant*, or Holy Island. According to Symeon, a monk of Durham, the island took its second name from the *Lindis*, a brook which empties itself into the sea from the opposite shore: "farn," the concluding syllable, is evidently a corruption of the Celtic word *fahren*, a recess. The more modern name was bestowed on it soon after the Conquest, with reference to the original sanctity of the place, and the sacred blood of monks and martyrs which had been shed by the Danes. The greatest distance of Lindisfarn from the coast scarcely exceeds two miles; it is, as Bede has properly described it, a semi-island, being twice an island and twice part of the continent in one day: at the flow of the tide it is encompassed by water, and at the ebb there is almost a dry passage both for horses and carriages. The depth of the water at ordinary high tides is about five, at spring-tides about seven feet. The path from the main land to the island at low water is a very precarious one, and is lengthened to about twice the actual distance between the two places by pools and quicksands, which have on too many occasions proved fatal to travellers;—the parish register affording numerous instances of the burials of persons found drowned in crossing the sands to the island. The intervening space presents at low water a dull and dreary appearance, the only objects to enliven the scene being an occasional fisherman, his wife, or children, slowly picking their way across the sands,—the rising of a flock of wild ducks, which they have disturbed,—or the silver wings of a sea-mew sparkling in the sun.

Holy Island measures, from east to west, about two miles and a quarter in length, and its breadth, from north to south, is scarcely a mile and a half. At the north-west part there runs out a slip of land of about a mile in length: the circumference of the entire island comprehends about eight miles. It contains about 1000 acres, above one-half of which is, from the violence of the tempests, covered with sand, and produces nothing but bents; even this part, however, is valuable as a rabbit warren: the remainder is enclosed and cultivated. The enclosures bear such good crops that the inhabitants seldom find it necessary to have recourse to the main land for their corn, or the other ordinary productions of the ground. The soil of Holy Island is divided into Crown lands, the possessions of the Dean and Chapter of Durham, and private freeholds. The principal proprietor is Mr. Henry Collingwood Selby, the Clerk of the Peace for Middlesex, who possesses nearly four-fifths of the island, partly by lease from the Crown, and partly in his right as a freeholder: this gentleman is also the lord of the manor. The island consists chiefly of one continuous plain, inclining to the south-west. The village stands upon an acclivity, which rises abruptly from the shore; and at the southern point of it there is a rock, of a conical figure, which rises almost perpendicularly to the height of sixty feet, and has on its lofty crown a small fortress, or castle. A little to the north-east of the village there are four caves, the longest of which is upwards of fifty feet long, and the entrance of which is just large enough to admit a man; over these caves a rock rises to the height of forty feet. The town or village of Holy Island consists of a few irregular narrow streets, the names of which are still preserved, although their importance has long departed, branching off from a small square called the Market Place. In the middle of this place, a few years ago, there stood the stump of an old market-cross, which was called the "Petting Stone," over which newly-married people were made to leap for luck. Modern improvement has, however, removed this remnant of ancient times, and erected in its place a handsome new cross of Norman character. The town contains about 100 houses, the great proportion of which are the humble cottages of the fishermen, who with their families constitute the chief part of the population (amounting to between 400 and 500 persons) of the island. There are very few good houses of ancient date; but the island having of late years become frequented as a bathing-place during the summer months, new ones have been erected, to be let out as lodgings for the accommodation of the visiters. Many of the fisherwomen's cottages are evidently of ancient date, not a few having in all probability witnessed the Priory in its glory; whilst in the more modern ones is to be seen here and there a window with stone stanchells, or an old weather-beaten oak-door, which prove themselves to have been part of the dismantled church. The old houses thus give to the town an air of antiquity, whilst those which have been more recently erected bestow on the whole place a neat and comfortable appearance. The shore is in many parts excellent for bathing, and the situation is both healthy and romantic. The north and east parts of the coast are formed of perpendicular rocks, and the other sides sink by gradual declinations towards the sea.

The castle, as we have before stated, stands upon a rock, and is accessible only by a winding pass cut on its southern side; it belongs to the crown, and is still looked on as a fortress by government, although it would avail little against any ship of considerable force: a few soldiers are generally stationed in it in connexion with the garrison of Berwick. Formerly its battery was mounted with seven or eight large guns, but these implements of war were removed by order of the War Office in the year 1819, and have not been since restored. The magnificence of the prospect from the walls cannot be surpassed; on the north the eye is arrested, after passing over an arm of the sea about seven miles in breadth, by the ancient and fortified town of Berwick; on the south, at about an equal distance, Bamborough Castle appears, elevated on a projecting promontory; towards the east there is an unlimited view of the sea, sometimes rough and gloomy, and at other times calm and resplendent, and scattered over with vessels; whilst on the west, after passing over the narrow channel by which the land is insulated, the shore exhibits for miles the rich and fertile districts of Islandshire and Norhamshire, ornamented with the seats of the descendants of the ancient border chiefs, the Haggerstons, the Ordes, the Askews, the Alders, &c., with their neat villages and accompanying woodlands. The antiquity of the castle is not accurately known; but a stronghold is known to have been erected where the present building stands in order to protect the monks from the incursions of the Danes. It was formerly of considerable importance, for, according to Rushworth (who was the Recorder of Berwick), it was seized by order of Parliament, during the civil war with Charles I., "it being of such consequence to the northern parts of the kingdom." During the rebellion of 1715 the seizure of this castle was

[Ruins of the Priory of Lindisfarn.]

planned and executed by two men only, friends of the Pretender, whose courage and sagacity would doubtless have entitled them to high honours had the cause been successful. The account is curious and interesting, and worthy of being more extensively known than it is. Lancelot Errington, a Catholic of ancient and respectable family, in Northumberland, but who himself was in comparatively reduced circumstances, having been promised assistance by Mr. Forster, the rebel general, moored a ship, of which he was master, in Holy Island harbour, and being well known in that part of the country, went, under pretence of wanting something, to the castle, the garrison of which consisted of a serjeant, a gunner, and ten men, and invited the serjeant and the men off duty on board his vessel. The invitation being accepted, he plied his guests so well with brandy that they were soon incapable of any opposition, and were secured. Lancelot, accompanied by his nephew, Mark Errington then returned to the castle, where they knocked down the two sentinels, surprised and turned out the gunner and three other soldiers, and shutting the gates, hoisted the Pretender's colours as a signal of success, and anxiously awaited the promised succour. Instead, however, of a reinforcement, a party of the king's troops arrived from Berwick, and the captors were obliged to retreat over the walls of the castle, hoping to conceal themselves among the seaweeds until it was dark; but the tide rising they were obliged to swim for their lives. They reached the rocks, in scrambling up which they were discovered and fired on; Lancelot having been wounded they were both taken and conveyed to Berwick gaol. Whilst thus confined, they managed to dig a burrow under the foundations of the prison, depositing the earth taken out in an old oven. Through this burrow they escaped, and having reached the Tweed, they actually rowed themselves across the river in the custom-house boat, which when done with was turned adrift. They reached Bamborough Castle, closely pursued by the soldiers; there they were concealed nine days in a pea-stack, a relative supplying them with food every night. With great difficulty they at last reached Sunderland, and got shipping for France. After the rebellion was suppressed, they took the benefit of the general pardon, and returned to Newcastle-upon-Tyne, where Lancelot died, in 1746, of grief on hearing of the victory of Culloden.

The early church history of Lindisfarn is the history of the see of Durham, a short sketch of which will be found in No. 73, p. 196. The bishopric of Lindisfarn was founded A.D. 634, and the island was the residence of fourteen bishops, among whom was the celebrated St. Cuthbert, whose miraculous powers, both in life and death, Bede, and the ancient chroniclers of the see of Durham, have celebrated in stories calculated for the age in which they lived. Towards the close of the tenth century, the see was removed, from the incursions of the Danes, to Chester le Street, and afterwards to Durham; and in the commencement of the following century, Lindisfarn, so long the residence of episcopacy, became the seat of the priory of Holy Island. This priory, interesting and beautiful in its decay, was erected about the year 1094, and belonged, down to the time of its dissolution, to the monks of the order of

St. Benedict. The Holy Island monks, like those inhabiting all the border monasteries, appear to have seen great prosperity, as well as much adversity; at one period rich with an income of 200*l.* per annum, at a time when such a sum was equivalent to 2000*l.* of the money of the present day; at another period their revenues were reduced to 32*l.* per annum, when the currency of the realm was in a state of great depreciation. After the removal of the see from the island, and from the establishment of the priory, the clergy of Lindisfarn lost the character they had before acquired for learning and piety. The antiquarian zeal of Mr. Raine has discovered that "their little library could at no period boast of a classical author, a chronicle, or one of Bede's numerous treatises; and it is a positive fact that from the year 1416 to the dissolution they were frequently, and in fact generally, without a bible. They had their service books for the church, some of which contained select portions of scripture as lessons, gospels, and epistles, to be periodically read and commented upon, and beyond them nothing more was necessary." After the dissolution of monasteries, the possessions of the priory were granted by Henry VIII. to the Dean and Chapter of Durham, to whom they still belong.

The Priory of Holy Island is, as might be supposed from the date of its erection, of the Norman style of architecture—

> "A solemn, huge, and dark red pile
> Placed on the margin of the isle."

In repairing the chancel about the year 1441, the monks having altered the form of the roof, fell into a great mistake in their chariness of buttresses for its support. The side walls being unable to resist the pressure of the roof, began to incline outwards, and the roof ultimately fell to the ground; these walls still stand leaning outwards in a singular manner. The church is in the form of a cross, the east and west limbs of which are still standing, while the other parts are totally in ruins and almost level with the ground. The tower of the church, which itself was the prototype of Durham Cathedral, stands in the centre, and was supported by two large arches, standing diagonally: one of them is yet standing, and from its extreme lightness and fine proportions, forms the most beautiful object in the ruins. The arch is somewhat similar to that of the stranger's hall at Canterbury. Hutchinson, in his 'View of Northumberland,' thus notices it —"These ruins retain at this day one most singular beauty; the tower has not formed a lantern, as in most cathedrals, but from the angles arches sprang crossing each other diagonally to form a canopy roof. One of these arches yet remains, unloaded with any superstructure, supported by the south-east and north-west corner pillars, and ornamented with the dancette or zigzag moulding, extending a fine bow over the chasm and heap of ruins occasioned by the falling in of the aisles." The whole structure was, unfortunately for the ornaments, built of a soft red freestone, the consequences of which have been noticed by Sir Walter Scott in 'Marmion.'

> "Not but the wasting sea-breeze keen
> Had worn the pillar's carving quaint,
> And mouldered in his niche the saint,
> And rounded with consuming power
> The pointed angles of each tower;
> Yet still entire the abbey stood,
> Like veteran, worn, but unsubdued."

This venerable ruin is, in despite of the exertions of the lord of the manor, fast disappearing; and in all probability before the lapse of another half century, the walls of it remaining will be level with the earth.

Upon a low detached portion of a basaltic line of rock in front of the ruins of the Priory Church, at about 100 yards distance from the main island, half an acre of which is covered with grass, is to be traced the outlines of a small chapel dedicated to St. Cuthbert; the walls in some places are two feet above the ground. The islet, which still bears the name of St. Cuthbert, is completely insulated at full tide.

The fishermen, who are the principal inhabitants of Holy Island, are a fine, athletic, hardy race of men. Each family possesses a small boat, in which the father and his sons, in all seasons of the year, however boisterous, go out in the middle of the night to fish. The coast abounds in cod, haddock, whitings, ling, and brat. The produce of the night's labour is conveyed in small carts, or on horseback in panniers, either to the neighbouring markets of Berwick or to the surrounding villages, where they are sold at very low prices; the finest haddocks for which the sea off Holy Island is famous, seldom bringing more than 3*d.* or 4*d.*, and not unfrequently selling for 1*d.* In thus disposing of their fish, these poor women will not unfrequently wander over a distance of twenty or thirty miles in a day, thinking themselves amply repaid if their whole stock produces one-half of what a London fishmonger charges for a single cod. The herring-fishing season is the Holy Island fishermen's harvest. Herring-fishing requires boats of a very large size, each of which is generally held in certain shares by several families, who join in the labour of fishing and the expenses of the boat. If the season be favourable, the produce of the herring-fishing is very considerable, and enables the fishermen to provide against the dull and profitless parts of the year. Many of the fishermen of Holy Island are the proprietors of the cottages in which they reside, as well as the small piece of ground which is generally attached to them.

SKETCHES OF THE PENINSULA.—No. IV.

Lisbon.

In our last paper we gave a sketch of the general appearance of Lisbon, and the impression which it makes on a visiter. We now conclude our notice of that city, by giving the following more detailed account of its buildings and general construction.

We have already mentioned its situation on the right or north bank of the Tagus, where it occupies, like ancient Rome, seven hills, the extremities of a mountain-range which traverses the entire province of Estramadura, in which Lisbon is situated. The ascent to the highest parts of the city is by a gradual slope, covered with irregular streets, though in some parts they are so steep as to render a descent, except on foot, extremely hazardous; while in others they are broad and spacious. After the great earthquake in 1755, which laid the entire city in ruins, the Marquis de Pombal, who was then Prime Minister, formed the design of rebuilding it on a regular plan. For this purpose, with the assistance of the ablest architects he could collect, he divided the ground into a number of squares, at equal distances from each other, subdividing the intervening space into streets, perfectly straight and parallel, and again dividing these by others at right angles. Only a very small part of this magnificent plan was carried into execution; and we can conceive, from that portion, what would have been the grandeur and magnificence of a city, situated as Lisbon is, and commanding so many excellent points of view, had it been thus rebuilt; but, as in London after the great fire, the opportunity was lost of erecting one of the most beautiful cities in the world, and it is to be hoped that such opportunities will not again occur. The Plaça do Commerçio (represented in our wood-cut in No. 340, as seen from the river) is one of Pombal's Squares, and was intended to form a kind of exchange for colonial and foreign merchants. The houses are of an equal height, *i. e.* two stories, and occupy three sides of the square, the fourth being open to the river. These three sides are surrounded by a piazza, under which business is conducted amongst the various merchants who assemble there. The custom-house, war offices, and national library occupy the upper chambers. In the centre stands the beautiful equestrian statue of King José, the figure and horse, as well as the serpents beneath his feet, are of bronze; the horse's eyes are said to have been formed of two splendid brilliants, and that Marshal Junot being unable to remove the statue, carried off these valuable eyes. The pedestal is formed of a single block of white marble, which is said to have required eighty yoke of oxen to draw it from the quarry. The front is ornamented with a bronze profile of the king, and the two sides are adorned with sculptures, representing the triumphs of Portugal in India and America. The whole is surrounded by an iron rail, supported at intervals by marble pillars, upon a platform ascended by about eight steps. The extreme elegance of this railing might serve as a model for imitation in this country, where the effect of our public statues is considerably decreased by the inelegance, if not absolute ugliness of the accessories. The quays or caes of Lisbon are upon a noble plan where finished, but, like the other parts of Pombal's design, are neglected and discontinued by a government that had not capacity to understand its beauty nor its utility. The principal landing-place is in the Plaça do Commerçio (perhaps better known as Black Horse Square), where the ascent from the river is formed by a magnificent flight of steps.

The three principal streets, Rua d'Oro, Rua de Plata, and Rua de Panño, so called from the trades carried on respectively in each, lead in parallel lines from Black Horse Square to the Rocio, a large and beautiful square, in which reviews of the troops, National Guard, &c., take place; the central window of what once was the Palace of the Inquisition, being fitted up for the royal reception. A little beyond are the public gardens, which, under the reign of the present queen, have been considerably enlarged. The beauty of these, as indeed of most foreign gardens, consists in a great number of trees and hedges cut into curious and grotesque figures, amongst which the corkscrew figure seems to be the favourite.

The Castle of St. George (the patron saint of Portugal, as of England) overlooks the Rocio, and the ascent to it is extremely toilsome. The streets leading up being so steep as in many places to be little more than one vast flight of steps. When, however, the summit is gained, the magnificence of the prospect amply recompenses the labour. The view is uninterrupted for leagues around on every side: to the north the horizon is bounded by the beautifully picturesque mountains of Cintra; following the line of coast, variegated with towns and villages and forts, we see the noble Tagus, guarded as it is by Belem and the Bouje, rolling its mighty stream into the boundless ocean; then from the plain green fields we see the houses deepen, street upon street follows, till all the city crowds upon the eye with its thousand domes, and convents, and palaces: as we turn to the southward, the precipices of Almada, crowned with the fort and tower, the deep bays of Moita and Alcoxete, the distant mountains of the Arabida, the isolated and castle-capped Palmella, combine to form a picture indescribably grand, and, as far as I have seen, unrivalled. The descent from the castle by the principal street is much more gradual than the ascent; and we here meet with the Limoeira or gaol for prisoners of all classes; and a little lower down the cathedral. This church, though extremely plain, and nearly destitute of any kind of ornament, has a noble and ancient appearance; the front consists of two towers, the space between them being occupied by the arched doorway and a circular window. The chapel of St. Antonio de Sé in its front adds considerably to the effect, as it relieves by its lavish ornament the plainness of the cathedral. There is a small fruit-market held here. Crowning the hill beyond the castle, stands the convent of St. Vicente de Fora, of which we have given an account and a view in No. 339. The suburbs of this division of Lisbon are extremely beautiful, being crowded with the quintas or villas of the nobility and gentry. These villas are the more numerous, as, save a trip to Cintra in the summer, few of the nobility leave the capital, even to visit their estates. Indeed, so small is the desire amongst the Portuguese to improve their property by agricultural means, that few have any idea of its condition, know its extent, or possess plans of even parts of their estates. Besides these mansions in the environs, many of the nobility possess splendid palaces in the heart of the city; such, indeed, is the palace of the Marquis de Quintilla, a little above the Caes do Soderé. There is little in the external appearance of this edifice to attract attention; but the interior is fitted up in the most splendid style, the furniture and ornaments being after the English fashion. The Marquis, who derives his immense wealth from the tobacco monopoly, is a great admirer of the English, and has several English servants. The chapel to the Quintilla Palace is, internally, very beautifully fitted up; there are a few good pictures in it, and the carvings around some of the shrines are very elegant. On the opposite side of the small square (Largo dasduas Igrejas) stands the Loretto, or Italian church; in the centre of the square there is a beautiful fountain, with a colossal statue of Neptune in white marble; higher up, and near the suburb of Val de Pereiro, stands the College of Nobles, founded in 1761, which is one of the three universities of Portugal, the other two being those of Coimbra and Evora.

THE ABBÉ DE L'EPÉE AND THE DEAF AND DUMB.

THE possibility of conveying instruction to the minds of the deaf and dumb began to be distinctly asserted in the sixteenth century. Rudolphus Agricola, of Groningen, mentioned that he had himself witnessed a person deaf from infancy, and consequently dumb, who had learned to understand writing, and, as if possessed of speech, was able to note down his thoughts. This statement was called in question; but "the theoretical principles on which the art rests were discovered and promulgated by the learned Jerome Cardan, of the University of Pavia, his native place. He was born in 1501, and died in 1576. Cardan thus expresses himself:—'Writing is associated with speech, and speech with thought; but written characters and ideas may be connected together without the intervention of sounds, as in hieroglyphic characters.'"

Pedro de Ponce, a monk of the order of St. Benedict, in Spain, who died in 1584, is stated to have been the first, or at least the most noted, amongst the early practitioners of the art of teaching the deaf and dumb. About forty years after the death of Ponce, John Paul Bonet, another Spaniard, to whom is attributed the merit of being the inventor of the one-handed alphabet, published a book on the subject. His work, which was in after-years useful to De l'Epée, is entitled 'Reduccion de las Lettras, y Arte para enseñar á hablar los Mudos.' During the time of Bonet, the art was also making some progress in Italy. Many first discoveries were probably made; several of them originated with, or were carried forwards by, philologists, and particularly among the schemers for an universal language. In England, John Bulwer's name must stand prior to that of any other individual as an author on the subject, and his views, as given in 'Philocophus,' are sound and practical. It has often been attempted to place Dr. Wallis at the head of this list of discoverers in England; but Bulwer's 'Philocophus, or the Deafe and Dumbe Man'

Friend,' was published several years before Wallis attempted even his treatise on speech, and he did not publish his claims as an instructor of the deaf till 1670*.

The Abbé de l'Epée holds a high rank amongst the friends and instructors of the deaf and dumb. Previous to his time, and during it, the art of teaching those labouring under this calamity was pursued more as a cunning craft, for the benefit of a few individuals who carefully concealed their modes of operation, than as a means of enabling men to alleviate one of the many natural evils to which our race are liable. The Abbé de l'Epée brought to the work a disinterested benevolence, an ingenuous frankness, a patient perseverance, which elevated the art into a profession honourable in itself, calculated to enlist men's sympathies, and to extend the will and the power of rescuing from mental oblivion those deprived of the usual means of communication with their fellows.

Charles Michel de l'Epée was born at Versailles in 1712. His father, who was the king's architect, was a clever and a good man, and brought up his family as all good men wish to do. Young De l'Epée was therefore fitly trained up. No scenes of domestic misery, arising from the indulgence of evil habits, passed before his eyes—his parents taught him the theory and showed him the practice of the fear of God and the love of his neighbour. He was educated for the church. Conscientious scruples stood in the way of his obtaining holy orders: being a Jansenist, he refused to sign a formulary of faith according to the established practice of the diocese of Paris, and he could not get past the rank of deacon. He therefore turned his attention to the law: but this profession did not suit his inclination and spirit. "His only desire was to be a minister of the gospel of peace, and at last he was successful." A nephew of the celebrated Bossuet, who, like his uncle, was a pious and liberal-minded man, being then Bishop of Troyes, ordained M. de l'Epée, and gave him a canonry in his cathedral-church.

The Abbé de l'Epée's attention was directed to the education of the deaf and dumb by an incidental circumstance. Business took him one day to a house where he found only two young women, who were busily engaged in needle-work. He spoke to them repeatedly, but received no answer. The mother arrived, and explained to him the cause of their silence—the two sisters were deaf and dumb! A kind ecclesiastic named Vanin, had tried to educate them by means of pictures; but after his death they were neglected. "Believing," says M. de l'Epée, "that these two children would live and die in ignorance of their religion, if I did not attempt some means of instructing them, I was touched with compassion, and told the mother that she might send them daily to my house, and that I would do whatever I might find possible for them."

M. de l'Epée recollected that when he was about sixteen years of age, his tutor, in a conversation he had with him, had proved to him that there is no more natural connexion between ideas and the sounds by which they are expressed to the ear, than between these same ideas and the written characters by which they are expressed to the eye. Thus, take any particular word, say *water* or *fire*:—the Englishman who hears these words spoken, or sees them in writing or in print, immediately associates the words with the things themselves, but to a foreigner ignorant of our language they convey no meaning at all. If ideas can be conveyed to the mind independently of sight or of sound, it follows that the blind can be taught to read by their fingers, and the deaf and dumb to speak by their hands, and to hear with their eyes. On this groundwork M. de L'Epée commenced, and devoted himself to the task of teaching the deaf and dumb. Some people thought him a fool for his pains, and ridiculed his labours, others pitied the infatuation of the good-natured enthusiast, vainly, as they imagined, trying to get access to minds shut up in prison. But neither sneers nor pity stopped the labours of the worthy Abbé. At last public opinion began to change; a clergyman said to him one day, "I formerly pitied you, I now pity you no longer; you are restoring to society and to religion beings who have been strangers to both."

"One day," says M. de l'Epée, "a stranger came to our public lesson, and offering me a Spanish book, said that it would be a real service to the owner if I would purchase it. I answered, that as I did not understand the language, it would be totally useless to me: but opening it casually, what should I see but the manual alphabet of the Spaniards neatly executed in copper-plate! I wanted no further inducement; I paid the messenger his demand, and kept the book. I then became impatient for the conclusion of the lesson; and what was my surprise when I found this title, 'Arte para enseñar á hablar los Mudos.' I had little difficulty to guess that this signified 'The Art of teaching the Dumb to speak,' and I immediately resolved to acquire the Spanish language for the benefit of my pupils." This book was Bonet's, already mentioned.

M. de l'Epée's attention was soon afterwards directed to another book, written in Latin, by John Conrad Amman, a Swiss physician, who resided at Haarlem, and who, in 1690, had undertaken the instruction of a girl, deaf and dumb from birth. These two works enabled him to form a system for himself, which, though it was deficient in real usefulness, as compared with the improvements since made in this department of instruction, was yet abundantly successful.

But M. de l'Epée did more than devote his time and labour to the instruction of the deaf and dumb. His income was about 400*l.* a year. Of this, he allowed about 100*l.* for his own expenses, and he "considered the remainder as the inheritance of his adopted children—the indigent deaf and dumb—to whose use it was faithfully applied. 'The rich,' says he, 'only come to my house by tolerance; it is not to them that I devote myself—it is to the poor: but for these I should never have undertaken the education of the deaf and dumb.' There was no kind of privation which he did not impose on himself, for the sake of his pupils. In order to supply their wants, he limited his own. So strictly did he adhere to the appropriation which he had made of his income, that in the rigorous winter of 1788, when suffering under the infirmities of age, he denied himself fuel, in order not to intrench upon the moderate sum to which he had confined his annual expenditure. All the remonstrances of his friends on this point were fruitless. His housekeeper having observed his rigid restriction, and doubtless imputing it to his real motive, led into his apartment his forty pupils, who conjured him to preserve himself for their sakes. He yielded not without difficulty to their persuasions, but afterwards reproached himself for this concession. Having exceeded his ordinary expenditure by about 300 livres (about 12*l.*) he would afterwards exclaim, in the midst of his pupils, 'My poor children, I have wronged you of an hundred crowns.'"

The Abbé, in his old age, and when the effects of his labours were too conspicuous to be reviled, received both approbation and flattery. The ambassador of Catherine of Russia offered him rich presents. "My lord," said the Abbé, "I never receive gold; tell her Majesty, that if my labours have appeared to her to claim her esteem, all that I ask is, that she will send

* See the 'Penny Cyclopædia,' article DEAF AND DUMB, for information on this interesting subject; and also the article DACTYLOLOGY, respecting manual alphabets. Engravings of manual alphabets have been given in the 'Penny Magazine,' vol. ii. p. 500. A portrait and memoir of the Abbé are also given in the 'Gallery of Portraits,' No. 29.

me a deaf and dumb person, or a master to be instructed in this art of teaching." When the emperor Joseph of Austria visited his institution, he expressed his astonishment that a man so deserving had not obtained at least an abbey, whose revenues he might apply to the wants of the deaf and dumb. He offered to ask one for him, or even to give him one in his own dominions. "I am already old," said M. de l'Epée; "if your Majesty wishes well to the deaf and dumb, it is not on *my* head, already bending to the tomb, that the benefit must fall—it is on the work itself."

The success of the Abbé de l'Epée was not complete, but he pursued his methods with openness and candour, and with the single desire of promoting the moral and intellectual advancement of the deaf and dumb. Heinecke of Leipzig, and Péreire of Paris, must be regarded as his rivals, but he invited them to a discussion of the merits of the various systems, which they declined While the good Abbé, with that frankness which formed a beautiful feature in his character, solicited the examination and the judgment of the learned upon his methods, his rivals shrouded their proceedings under a veil of mystery. The Abbé devoted his life and whole fortune, excepting a bare supply for his own wants, to the service of the class whom he had taken under his protection. Péreire refused to disclose his methods except for a large recompense; and Heinecke, in addition to receiving payment from the rich, had 400 crowns annually allowed him by the grand duke of Saxony. Both these persons made the art they professed an interested speculation; the Abbé de l'Epée only tolerated the rich; he was proud of being the instructor of the indigent. His successor, the Abbé Sicard, carried forward the principles of De l'Epée; he instructed his pupils in the elements of composition, a branch of their education comparatively new, and in which Sicard most completely evinced his superiority over his master. Sicard at first conducted a school at Bordeaux; on the death of the Abbé de l'Epée he was called to fill his place at Paris.

The Abbé de l'Epée died on the 23rd of December, 1789. Various honours were paid to his memory; the king's preacher pronounced his funeral oration; and one of his deaf and dumb pupils wrote a distich to be placed under the bust of his teacher:—

"Il révèle a la fois secrets merveilleux,
De parler par les mains, d'entendre par les yeux."

The article already referred to, in the 'Penny Cyclopædia,' on the DEAF and DUMB (from which a portion of the preceding information has been taken), contains the following statement:—

"There are 8000 deaf mutes in England; the institutions at present in operation are not capable of educating more than 600. It is calculated that at least one-eighth of the whole number are within the age and other qualifications generally prescribed for education. It therefore seems necessary that more extended provisions should be made for their instruction."

[Portrait of the Abbé de l'Epée.]

∴ The Office of the Society for the Diffusion of Useful Knowledge is at 59, Lincoln's Inn Fields.
LONDON:—CHARLES KNIGHT & CO., 22, LUDGATE STREET.
Printed by WILLIAM CLOWES and SONS, Stamford Street.

Monthly Supplement of
THE PENNY MAGAZINE
OF THE
Society for the Diffusion of Useful Knowledge.

342.] June 30 to July 31, 1837.

ENGLISH LAKES.

[Concluded from No. 336.]

[Skiddaw, from the southern end of Lake Derwentwater.]

From Bout a rough mountain path traverses the moors to Wastdale Head, passing a cheerless sheet of water called Burnmoor Tarn, between Scawfell and the Screes. Near the way-side the stream which runs down to Bout forms a cascade, bare and unadorned by enclosing precipices, yet possessing a character of grandeur, at all events when swollen by recent rains*. The path leads high over the southern shoulder of Scawfell, and then descends down a steep peat track into Upper Wastdale, a little above the lake. The stranger, wishing to see Wastwater, must not attempt to pass along the side of the Screes, as the hill is called which forms the southern side of the lake, from a provincial term signifying a crumbling slope of loose materials. Here the declivity is so steep, and the slaty soil so incoherent, that it is commonly said to be impossible to pass along it; and the attempt would certainly be attended with danger. The views obtained by going along the top of the Screes are said to be very fine. There is a hamlet called Strands, a mile below the foot of Wastwater, where the traveller will find quarters for the night: there is nothing to induce him to proceed farther towards the sea, except the ruin of Calder Abbey, which is small but pretty.

Within some half an hour's walk from Strands is a remarkable spot, called Haul-gill, or else Hollow-gill. It is a deep ravine at the south-west foot of the Screes, among granite rocks, which, by the decomposition of their felspar, have been wasted into abrupt peaks and precipices—a sort of miniature mimicry of the *aiguilles* of Chamouni. This is one of the most curious and striking things in the whole district: it is a good place for ascending the Screes from Nether Wastdale (as the valley below the lake is called) for those who have good nerves. There is a very beautiful vein of spicular iron here; also some fine hœmatite. These particulars are derived from a friend: I am not aware that this object has ever before been pointed out to the attention of travellers.

There is a simplicity and severity about Wastwater not to be found in any of its neighbour lakes, except perhaps that of Ennerdale, which is equally destitute of the cheerfulness imparted by cultivation, but inferior in

* This is not mentioned in the guide-books which I have at hand. I understood it to be called Buck- (pronounced Bouk-) Pot, probably from a resemblance which the deep circular basin into which the water falls may be fancied to bear to a huge washing-tub. *Buck* is an old English word, synonymous with wash; as in the 'Merry Wives of Windsor,' act iii, scene 3, where Falstaff is hidden in a *buck-basket*, "You were best meddle with *buck*-washing."

the height and ruggedness of its mountain boundaries. Yet at Wastwater, on a bright day, there is no want of cheerfulness: the sides of the Screes, streaked with brilliant hues of red and brown, like the changeable colours of a pigeon's neck, are beautiful in themselves, and contrast well with the grassy slopes of the northern side. At the head of the lake the mural precipices of Scawfell rise near 3000 feet above the eye, and rival the grandest scenes of the Scottish Highlands. Not far above the lake, between Yewbarrow and Kirkfell, lies Mosedale, closed to the north by the Pillar. This is one of our loftier mountains, 2893 feet in height; and, being composed, like Scawfell, of the hard slate of the middle formation, it presents to Ennerdale a far grander front than is afforded by the soft shale of Skiddaw, or even by the bolder precipices of Saddleback or Helvellyn *.

The path up Mosedale, crossing a slack called Black Sail, between the Pillar and Kirkfell, descends a rough hill-side into Gillerthwaite, as the upper part of Ennerdale is called. A scene of more entire seclusion can hardly be imagined. Not a sign of human life or labour meets the eye. The head of the dale is closed by Kirkfell and Gavel, and on the opposite side High Stile and Red Pike part it from Buttermere. Fording the river, we pursue the way to Buttermere over a second lofty pass to the east of High Stile, called Scarf Gap; cross the infant stream of the Cocker by a bridge, and traversing a marshy but cultivated flat, reach a beaten road again at the farm of Gatesgarth, two miles from Buttermere inn and church. This route, from Strands to Buttermere, includes as much variety and beauty as can well be crowded into a four hours' walk. A horse may be taken over it in dry weather, but as the hills are both soft and rough, it will be prudent to obtain the help of a guide. Those who can walk will find walking quicker and pleasanter than riding; indeed a good deal of the ground must be done on foot.

About a mile of ground lies between Buttermere and Crummock-water, which is near four miles long. Melbreak lies on the west, and on the east Grasmoor, the principal mountain of the cluster which separates this vale from that of Keswick. About half a mile from the head of the lake a torrent runs into it on the western side, on which is Scale Force, the highest waterfall in the country. Small as the stream is, except in time of flood, it has eaten a deep ravine into the mountain. The upper fall is an unbroken shoot, of which the height is said to be 156 feet: after circling in a small basin, the water escapes by a second fall of thirty or forty feet, and hurries down to the lake about a mile distant. The usual way of visiting it is by boat from Scale Hill or Buttermere: there is however a footpath from the village of Buttermere to the lower part of Ennerdale, which goes close to the fall, and afterwards past Floutern Tarn. This will suit persons who wish to see only the best part of Ennerdale. Quitting the path near Floutern Tarn, they may strike the lake about its centre, and either follow Gillerthwaite to the passes already described, or go direct over the Pillar into Mosedale, and so to Strands.

A curious tarn, the stream from which is seen foaming down the hill-side in a succession of falls, lies above Buttermere, deep set in a hollow between Red Pike and High Style.

A third small lake, called Lowes-water, to the north of Melbreak, combines with Buttermere and Crummock to form the Cocker river, which runs into the Derwent at Cockermouth, where there are extensive remains of the ancient castle. There is a good inn at Scale Hill, near the foot of Crummock-water (where boats can be procured to go up the lake), distant from Keswick twelve miles by way of Lorton and the old road over the pass of Whinlatter. In the churchyard of Lorton is a remarkable yew-tree,

"——— pride of Lorton Vale,
Which to this day stands single, in the midst
Of its own darkness, as it stood of yore,
Not loth to furnish weapons for the bands
Of Umfraville or Percy, ere they march'd
To Scotland's heaths: or those that cross'd the sea
And drew their sounding bows at Azincour;
Perhaps at earlier Crecy, or Poictiers.
Of vast circumference, and gloom profound,
This solitary tree, a living thing,
Produced too slowly ever to decay
Of form and aspect too magnificent
To be destroy'd *."

A country road which runs along the skirts of Whinlatter, leaving Lorton to the west, will considerably shorten the distance, on foot or horseback, from Scale Hill to Keswick.

Between Wastwater and the lower part of Ennerdale lies an extensive, desolate tract of moor and mountain The hills attain no great height, and possess little interest.

Keswick stands upon a gentle slope, not half a mile from the lower end of Derwentwater. By the census of 1831 the township contained 2159 inhabitants; of whom a considerable number is employed in the manufacture of woollen goods, pencils, &c. The town possesses two museums, Crosthwaite's and Hutton's, and there is an exhibition of views of the Lakes, painted by a clever artist, some time since deceased, named Green; who was perhaps more thoroughly acquainted with all the windings of the country than any other man, and wrote a Guide in two octavo volumes, which is the most minute description extant of the country. The river Greta, issuing from St. John's Vale, skirts the base of Latrigg, a round-backed eminence to the south of Skiddaw, and passes at the back of the town, supplying water-power for the various manufactories: at the end of the main street it is crossed by a bridge, and hastens to join the Derwent, near the point where the latter issues from the lake. Their united streams are crossed by a substantial two-arched bridge, a mile from Keswick, on the road to Cockermouth. The lake acts as a reservoir, and prevents the river from becoming low, except after long droughts; and on a hot day, its clear, glancing, rapid stream will tempt the wayfarer to linger here. It runs on through an alluvial flat, about three miles long, to Bassenthwaite. A foot-path, not very easily followed by the stranger, traverses the fields on its western bank, and crossing the river about a mile above Bassenthwaite-water, leads into the road from Keswick to Wigton.

At the village of Portinscale, just beyond the bridge above mentioned, the road round Derwentwater turns off from the Cockermouth road. After skirting the green hill called Swinside, and the woods of Waterend, lately the property of Lord William Gordon, it crosses the broad opening of Newlands, and ascending a steep short hill, passes at a considerable height along the open side of Catbells, commanding one of the best views of the lake and valley. Crossing the river at the village of Grange, the road back towards Keswick lies under a romantic line of crags, feathered with birch and mountain ash. A public-house, distant one mile from Grange, warns us that we have reached the celebrated fall of Lodore, which lies immediately at the back of the premises; and access (which is most conveniently obtained through the inn garden) used not to be very graciously granted unless an offering were made "for the good of the house." This celebrated cataract is in fact a succession of small distinct falls, down a long

* ——— "It wears the shape
Of a vast building made of many crags;
And in the midst is one particular crag,
Which rises like a column from the vale,
Whence by our shepherds it is called The Pillar."—
Wordsworth's 'Brothers.'

* Wordsworth's 'Yew Trees.

gully, half choked with fallen rocks; and as the broken threadlike streamlets bear no proportion to the vastness of the ravine, the first sensation of those who come here to see a *waterfall* is likely to be disappointment. Occasionally, in thaws and sudden floods, the torrent sweeps with an unbroken front over all these obstacles; but the flush of water soon subsides. On either side, walls of rock rise to an unusual height, thickly clothed below, and fringed above with the usual native growth of ash and birch. When the water is low, it is very possible to pass up the chasm to the level of the upper valley, which, however, may be at all times more easily attained by a circuitous path a little to the south of the inn. The view of Derwentwater, backed by Skiddaw, looking from above, through the chasm, is very fine, and has been a favourite subject with artists.

Barrow, the residence of Mr. Pocklington, is a mile nearer Keswick: it is surrounded by fine old trees, and has within the grounds a waterfall, of scanty volume but considerable height, within a few yards of the back of the house, and in full view of the windows. After passing under Walla Crag, we come, a mile from Keswick, to an insulated woody knoll, called Castlelet, which is much visited, as lying within easy distance, and commanding an excellent view up and down the valley. Another favourite short walk is to Friars' Crag, a low bluff point, opposite to Derwent Island. The circuit of the lake, by the carriage-road, is twelve miles.

Lord's Island, the largest in the lake, situated perhaps an hundred yards from the shore, under Walla Crag, was the stronghold of the powerful family of Ratcliffes, Earls of Derwentwater, whose possessions, it need hardly be said, were forfeited after the Rebellion of 1715, and transferred to Greenwich Hospital. The property round Keswick was lately sold, and now belongs to Mr. Marshall of Hallsteads, on Ullswater. The ancient seat of the Ratcliffes has long perished; and the island is occupied by a melancholy phalanx of spindling fir-trees. The same ill-fortune has overtaken St. Herbert's Island, which formerly boasted a noble growth of venerable oaks: here St. Herbert, the contemporary and friend of St. Cuthbert in the seventh century, is said to have fixed his hermitage. Derwent (or, as it was formerly called, having belonged to Fountains Abbey, Vicars) Island is occupied by the house and grounds of General Peachy, and richly wooded with chesnut, beech, and various kinds of pine, chiefly planted by the present proprietor. The trees have thriven remarkably, and attained an amplitude of girth and luxuriance of foliage, such as rarely gladden the planter's eye. There are three or four more islands, or islets, (Rampsholm, Lingholm, &c.) which are beautiful in themselves; but their number gives an unpleasant spottiness to the lake when viewed from a height. The celebrated Floating Island, near the south-eastern corner of the lake, is a portion of the peaty bottom, which, from some cause not very clearly explained, occasionally rises to the surface. The most probable supposition is, that the mass is swollen and buoyed up by gas, produced by the decomposition of vegetable matter. On piercing it with a boat-hook, gas (carbureted hydrogen and azote) issues in abundance.

Almost all the lakes and streams of the country are remarkable for the extreme limpidity, purity, and softness of their waters, which render them most delightful to the swimmer. In these qualities the lakes and river of this vale are pre-eminent.

Behind the village of Grange, in the gorge of Borrowdale, rises a high and nearly detached rock, called Castle Crag, the site of an ancient fortification, supposed to be Roman, of which the traces are now obliterated by the working of the slate quarry. On the western side, the bed of the river alone separates it from the opposing hills; and through this narrow pass the road from Keswick into Borrowdale runs. It is the most picturesque part of this most lovely valley. A new road has been cut lately, near the bed of the river, avoiding the ups and downs of the old way, which led past the celebrated Bowder Stone, the largest known detached fragment of rock in Britain. Which is the more beautiful it is hard to say: I should recommend the old road in going *up* the valley on foot or horseback, and the new one in going *down* it. Beyond the hamlet of Rosthwaite (where there is a small house of entertainment, the last in the valley), six miles from Keswick, the valley divides into two branches, that to the left being called Stonethwaite, that to the right, Seathwaite. Following the latter, which is the principal, we come, two miles from Rosthwaite, to a large substantial farmhouse, called Seatollar, by which a rough mountain-road diverges to the right, and, passing under Honister Crag, descends upon Buttermere. A mile beyond Seatollar the Black-lead (or, as it is provincially termed, "Wad") Mine indicates its position, high on the hill-side, by those unsightly heaps of rubbish which always attend mining operations. The mineral is found pure and fit for market; and, in consequence of the temptation to plunder afforded by its value* and small bulk, is not allowed to be sold on the spot: the whole produce is barrelled, and sent up to the warehouse of the proprietors in London. Under the mine, and rather nearer to Seatollar, a dark spot is seen in the copsewood, which thus far clothes the hill. These are the celebrated Borrowdale Yews, four in number, not to mention some smaller ones. Among them one is pre-eminent, which, being in the vigour of its age, and undecayed, ranks among the finest specimens of its kind in England †. The Lorton Yew is larger, and that in Patterdale churchyard may equal or exceed this in size;—but they have lost the mighty limbs, and dark umbrageous foliage, contrasting so well with the rich chesnut-coloured trunk, which are here still to be seen in mature perfection. Mr. Wordsworth, in his 'Yew Trees,' after commemorating that of Lorton, continues,

"Worthier still of note
Are those fraternal Four of Borrowdale,
Join'd in one solemn and capacious grove;
Huge trunks!—and each particular trunk a growth
Of intertwisted fibres serpentine
Up-coiling, and inveterately convolved,—
Nor uninform'd with Phantasy, and looks
That threaten the profane;—a pillar'd shade,
Upon whose grassless floor of red-brown hue,
By sheddings from the pining umbrage tinged
Perennially—beneath whose sable roof
Of boughs, as if for festal purpose, deck'd
With unrejoicing berries, ghostly Shapes
May meet at noontide—Fear and trembling Hope,
Silence and Foresight—Death the Skeleton,
And Time the Shadow,—there to celebrate,
As in a natural temple scatter'd o'er
With altars undisturb'd of mossy stone,
United worship; or in mute repose
To lie, and listen to the mountain-flood
Murmuring from Glaramara's ‡ inmost caves."

At the hamlet of Seathwaite wood and cultivation end: the road, now reduced to a horse-track, follows the rapidly-ascending bed of the stream for a mile farther, and then, turning sharp over a little bridge, thrown across that branch of the Grange river which comes

* The better qualities have formerly been worth from thirty to forty shillings a pound: what may be the present value, to the proprietors, we do not know.

† The Ankerwyke Yew, near Staines, exceeds it in size, and may equal it in beauty, if still in the condition described in the 'Penny Cyclopædia,' article AGE OF TREES. This tree is said to have been in existence in the reign of King John. Norbury Park, near Leatherhead, contains a number of enormous yews which Fuseli called the Grove of the Furies. The impressive situation in which the Borrowdale Yews stand no doubt adds much to their effect.

‡ A part of the Borrowdale Fells, above Rosthwaite, between Seathwaite and Langstreth.

2 P 2

down from Ash Course, begins immediately to mount Sty Head. But Stockley Bridge, as it is called, will detain our attention for a time, as a perfect miniature model of a bridge and waterfall. It is a rough stone arch, apparently wedged rather than cemented together, hardly two yards in span, or one in breadth, with no parapet except a slight elevation of the outer stones on either side, between which there seems hardly room for a horse to plant his feet. It is thrown over a rocky cleft, ten or twelve feet above the stream, with a small glittering cascade above, and a sea-green pool below; for the purest spring is not more free from taint of moss, than the water which descends from these hills. Small as it is, this is one of the most perfect specimens left of those *native* bridges, the gradual disappearance of which Mr. Wordsworth laments*.

The height of Sty Head above the valley is said by Mr. Baines ('Companion to the Lakes') to be 1250 feet: this, however, is its height above the sea; its height above Stockley Bridge probably does not exceed 750 or 800 feet. At the top of the first ascent is a small plain, in which lies a narrow sheet of water, called Sty Head Tarn. Beyond it, the road still rises, until turning a sharp point of rock, with a chasm at our feet, Wastdale lies in view more than a thousand feet below; while in front the precipices of the Pikes rise double that height. The grandeur of the scene is enhanced by the suddenness with which it comes into view, and by a nervous sensation which the stranger, especially if on horseback, will be likely to experience; for he seems to hang over the precipice, so narrow is the path that winds among the crags which here crest the declivity. On the Wastdale side of Gavel garnets abound in the hard flinty slate.

Sty Head Tarn is fed by a rill from Sprinkling Tarn, the source of one branch of the Grange river, which lies some hundred feet higher, under the broad front of Great End. To Sprinkling Tarn, or with care, even to Ash Course, horses may be taken in the ascent of the Pikes. Passing south of the tarn, we proceed eastward up the hill-side towards Ash Course, where this route unites with the shorter and more direct one, which follows the water up from Stockley Bridge. Leaving Great End behind, we soon gain the ridge of the mountain, at an elevation not much inferior to that of the Pikes themselves; but two or three deep hollows are to be crossed before we reach the highest point, which is distinguished by a lofty pile of stones and wood. Such piles of stone are raised by the country-people on every prominent point, almost without exception, and called *men*: this one, however, having been raised for the trigonometrical survey, is of unusual height, and is surmounted by three tall fir-poles, bound together, which, from the vale below, look like a single walking-stick. These ups and downs are very tantalising, for most persons have had enough of climbing by the time they have come thus far; and the more so, as the walking is laborious, the top of the mountain, from Great End to the Pikes, being covered by a mass of angular disjointed blocks, and those not always steady under foot. Much care is necessary, for a slip into the interstices, or a fall among their sharp angles, might very easily lead to a broken bone, which would be peculiarly inconvenient here. The last hollow is the deepest; and as we rest on its edge, the opposite ascent seems almost perpendicular. Yet all, even of the lady visiters (few enough in number) who come this way, will muster up strength enough for the last climb, severe as it is, which is to place them on the highest English mountain, and that one which commands the noblest view. None even of the loftier Scottish mountains, which I have been able to ascend, is equal in this respect. Much of its grandeur it owes to being environed by mountains of almost equal height,—to the north Great End and Gavel, to the east Bowfell, to the south Scawfell. Beyond and between them countless peaks and ridges extend on all sides, except to the west, where is stretched the vast expanse of the Irish Sea. On either side the precipices which descend into Eskdale and Wastdale appear of fearful depth; indeed, the finest object in this sublime view is perhaps the precipice of the sister mountain of Scawfell. The whole coast, from Anglesey to the Mull of Galloway is visible; half way between which rise the lofty hills of the Isle of Man; and in days of extraordinary clearness, such as that in which the writer first stood here—one of those rare days, when there is neither haze in the air, nor cloud in the sky, when the sea puts on its deepest azure, and every wave dances and sparkles in the sun—the blue hills of Ireland may be dimly seen.

"On the summit of the Pike," says Mr. Wordsworth, "which we gained after much toil, though without difficulty, there was not a breath of air to stir even the papers containing our refreshment as they lay spread out upon a rock. The stillness seemed not to be of this world; we paused and kept silence to listen, and no sound could be heard; the Scawfell cataracts were voiceless to us, and there was not an insect to hum in the air. The vales which we had seen from Ash-course lay still in view; and side by side with Eskdale we now saw the sister vale of Donnerdale terminated by the Duddon sands. But the majesty of the mountains below and close to us is not to be conceived. We now beheld the whole mass of Great Gavel from its base—the Den of Wastdale at our feet—a gulph immeasurable: Grassmoor, and the other mountains of Crummock—Ennerdale and its mountains—and the sea beyond. We sat down to our repast, and gladly would we have tempered our beverage (for there was no spring or well near us) with such a supply of delicious water as we might have procured, had we been on the rival summit of Great Gavel; for on its highest point is a small triangular receptacle in the native rock, which the shepherds say is never dry. There we might have slaked our thirst plenteously with a pure and celestial liquid; for the cup or basin, it appears, has no other feeder than the dews of heaven, the showers, the vapours, the hoar-frost, and the spotless snow.

"Round the top of Scawfell Pike not a blade of grass is to be seen. Cushions or tufts of moss, parched and brown, appear between the huge blocks and stones that lie in heaps on all sides to a great distance, like skeletons or bones of the earth not needed at the creation, and there left to be covered with never-dying lichens, which the clouds and dews nourish, and adorn with colours of vivid and exquisite beauty. Flowers, the most brilliant feathers, and even gems, scarcely surpass in colouring some of those masses of stone, which no human eye beholds, except the shepherd or traveller be led thither by curiosity."

Scawfell is separated from the Pikes by a deep chasm, called Mickledoor, at the bottom of which a narrow ridge, like the roof of a house, slopes into Eskdale on

* 'Scenery of Lakes,' p. 53. "To the smallness of the several properties is owing the great number of bridges over the brooks and torrents, and the daring and graceful neglect of danger or accommodation with which so many of them are constructed, the rudeness of the forms of some, and their endless variety. But when I speak of this rudeness, I must at the same time add, that many of these structures are in themselves models of elegance, as if they had been formed upon principles of the most thoughtful architecture. It is to be regretted that these monuments of the skill of our ancestors, and of that happy instinct by which consummate beauty was produced, are disappearing fast: but sufficient specimens remain to give a high gratification to the man of genuine taste. Travellers who may not have been accustomed to pay attention to things so inobtrusive will excuse me if I point out the proportion between the span and elevation of the arch, the lightness of the parapet, and the graceful manner in which its curve follows faithfully that of the arch."

[Fall on the Brook which runs from Sty Head Tarn into Borrowdale.]

one side, and into Wastdale on the other. So far all is easy; but the ascent of Scawfell from this point ought not to be undertaken without a guide well acquainted with the practicable passes of this mountain. It is encompassed by precipices, varied with narrow terraces of turf, and slanting sheets of naked rock; and a stranger might chance to find himself entrapped into some place, where to go backwards or forwards would be equally difficult and dangerous. Never having had a guide on the Pikes, and thinking it inexpedient to try my chance alone, I never faced the climb from Mickledoor upwards. For the following account I am indebted to a friend:—"There are two ways from Mickledoor to Scawfell—one is on the east side of Scawfell. I could not persuade my guide, a shepherd of Upper Wastdale, to conduct me by it; the other, on the north face of Scawfell I went by. It is *very* laborious, and looks dangerous; but, in fact, there is no risk except that of a sprained ankle. It is through the Lord's Rake, a shaft between two vertical walls of rock, about five yards across all the way up, and twenty or twenty-five minutes' hard climbing on all fours up a slope of about 45°. The place must have been cut out by a water-course; but it is now dry and covered with light shingle. It looks right down into Hollow Stones (the deep vale between the Pikes and Scawfell), and most fearful it does look; but it is not dangerous. When we reached the inn at Eskdale, over Scawfell, my shepherd was very proud of having brought me through the Lord's Rake, and the people were much surprised. It seems to be rather a feat in the country. It is the strangest place I ever saw. I think there is no indication of it from the outside. It may be recommended to all who can bear hard labour, and enjoy the appearance of danger without the reality."

If the traveller be bound from the Pikes into Eskdale, a direct and practicable descent may be found by way of Mickledoor; or a tolerably straight course may be shaped from the Pikes either into Wastdale or, if the traveller be returning to Keswick, back to Sty Head by the western side of the mountain, leaving Great End to the right, and keeping farther down the hill-side than would at first seem necessary, to avoid some deep and apparently impassable ravines, which run out from among the crags of Great End. These oblige him to descend below the level of Sty Head.

From Ash Course, an hour well used will take the walker, in a different direction, to the head of Langdale. the way lies past Angle Tarn, under the northern precipice of Bowfell. The best descent into Langdale is down a steep rugged gully, called Rosset Gill. The circuit from Keswick to Ambleside by Sty Head, the Pikes, Ash Course, and Langdale, may be reckoned at thirty miles, and lies throughout among the finest scenery of the country.

Stonethwaite, the eastern division of Borrowdale, is subdivided into two branches, of which the eastern, called Greenup, leads into the fells towards the head of Easdale, and so communicates with Grasmere; while the Langstreth, which is the principal branch, turns south, and running parallel to Seathwaite, is closed by the precipice which towers over Angle Tarn, the head of this branch of the Derwent. The high rock which terminates the range of hills between Langstreth and Greenup is called Eagle Crag. The lower part of Seathwaite is beautifully wooded. Langstreth lies high, and is of wilder character. Little wood remains in it; but the scattered hollies, left here and elsewhere in former times to furnish winter browsing for the sheep, testify to the once sylvan aspect of the dale. About three miles up, a gill dashes down the hill-side from the left, and a sheep-pen marks its point of junction with the main stream. Here the ill-tracked path turns away from the main valley, to cross the lofty pass called the Stake into Langdale. Steep, green, and zigzag, distinguishable from the rest of the hill-side chiefly by the closeness and fresh green of the turf, it follows the stream, sometimes in perilous proximity, and ushers us upon a boggy moor, a mile perhaps in extent; on crossing which, we commence a still steeper, rougher, and longer descent into Langdale, leaving to the left the western Langdale pike, called Pike of Stickle. Here we return to ground which has been already described.

One of the most interesting excursions from Keswick is the circuit by Newlands, Buttermere and Borrowdale. South of Swinside the road to Buttermere turns away from that which encircles the lake, and skirting Cawsey Pike begins to ascend Newlands. The principal hills on the opposite side are called Hindscarth and Robinson Crag. The descent into Buttermere is steep and long, as has been said before; and the road runs, at a height alarming to weak nerves, above the ravine which separates this from the opposite hill, called Whitelees. Soon after passing Gatesgarth we begin to ascend again, leaving to the south Honister Crag, which rises 1500 feet above the vale of Buttermere. Here slate quarries have been extensively worked. A deep depression in the Borrowdale fells conducts us to Seatollar, four miles from Gatesgarth and eight from Keswick. The pass from Buttermere to Borrowdale is just practicable for a car or cart, but very fatiguing from the roughness of the road. Those, more especially, who can neither walk nor ride over the loftier passes will find their account in traversing this noble route. The whole day's journey is estimated at twenty-three miles.

The stream which forms the waterfall of Lodore comes from a small upland valley called Watendlath, well worth a visit. The hamlet of that name is on the border of a beautiful circular little lake, about two miles from Lodore; the road thither from Keswick turns from the lake side beyond Walla Crag, and passes just behind Barrow House. A pretty rustic bridge crosses the stream where it issues from the tarn, and leads over the Borrowdale fells to Rosthwaite. This is a very pleasant morning's ride from Keswick; it may be varied, on foot, by turning to the left instead of the right at Watendlath, and crossing the Wythburn fells to Thirlmere, also called Leatheswater, distant about four miles from Watendlath, over rough, heathery, trackless hills, which on a fine day, especially when the heath is in blossom, make a wild and delightful walk. Thirlmere, a long, dark, narrow lake, is nearly cut in two by two opposite capes, joined by a wooden bridge. The water here is commonly fordable for horses. Near the sixth milestone from Keswick a track leads from the high-road to this point, and the traveller from Ambleside will do well to follow it for the sake of seeing the lower, and far most beautiful, part of the lake, which is hidden from the high-road by an intervening wooded hill, called the How. The black high rock, like a round tower, at the end of the lake, is Raven Crag. We rejoin the turnpike road on Shoulthwaite Moss, four miles from Keswick, having missed nothing by the diversion (which does not lengthen the way more than a mile), except the view down the vale of St. John, through which, after issuing from Thirlmere, the Greta flows, with its Castle Rock and long vista of crags, closed by the precipices of Saddleback. This is the scene of Scott's pretty poem, the 'Bridal of Triermain. The low rocky hill which intervenes between Shoulthwaite Moss and St. John's Vale is called Naddle (or more properly Nathdale) Fell. Soon after crossing the moss the road begins to mount a long hill called Castlerigg, from the brow of which a noble view over the vale of Keswick expands before us. This is the prospect of which Gray speaks in such rapturous terms.

The ascent of Skiddaw is long but easy: a lady may ride to the top and down again without even dismounting. It is the fourth English mountain in height, being 3022 feet above the sea, and 2800 above the lake of Bassenthwaite, which lies close at its foot. In respect of view, it is inferior to several points of smaller height, owing to its position nearly on the outside of the mountain district, and the absence of crags and precipices on the mountain itself. The gradual opening of the vale of Keswick, as we ascend, is however extremely beautiful; and the view is finer three quarters up, than on the summit. To the north and east a large tract of low moor extends; and the northern distance also is tame and level. The top of Skiddaw is formed by a ridge, which runs north and south about half a mile, with no great difference of elevation. The highest point visible from Keswick and Derwentwater is not the summit, but the southern end of this ridge.

I once witnessed with three companions an atmospheric phenomenon on this mountain, rare in England, but not unfamiliar it is said on the Hartz mountains in Germany, where its occurrence is supposed to have given rise to the superstitious legends of the Giant of the Brocken. We set out late in a fine August night to reach the top of Skiddaw before sunrise: there was no moon, but the stars shone brilliantly, and as we rose up the steep hill-side overhanging Applethwaite, the lake and valley became slowly more and more distinct in the cold leaden hue of early twilight. As often happens after the finest nights, the floating vapours were suddenly condensed, and by the time we reached the table-land near the top, we were enveloped in a thick white mist, cold and uncomfortable, which confined our sight to a circle of a few yards diameter. Suddenly the white fog took a beautiful rose colour, produced probably, like the last hues of evening, by the greater refractive power of the red rays, as the first beams of the sun shot above the horizon. This very soon vanished. One of the party was a short distance in advance, when a ray of sunshine darted through the mist, and he saw a figure walking ten or fifteen yards distant from his side. Taking it for granted that this was one of his companions, whom he had supposed at some distance, he vented some expression of disappointment; and receiving no answer, repeated and repeated it again. Still there was no answer, though the figure kept steadily advancing with even steps. At last he stopped, half angry, and turned quite round to look at his silent companion, who did the same, but receded as he approached; and it became evident that the figure, apparently dimly seen through the mist, was his own shadow reflected on it. It was then surrounded by a bright halo, and as the light became stronger, grew less and less distinct. The rest of the party came up in time to witness this remarkable appearance with some modification. On reaching the ridge of the mountain, our figures, of super-human size, appeared to be projected on the mist in the direction of the Solway.

The tract of moor which lies between Skiddaw and Saddleback, bounded by High Pike and Carrock on the north, is called Skiddaw Forest; it is traversed by the upper part of the Caldew river. In Bowscale Fell, as the northern part of the great mass of Saddleback is called, lies Bowscale Tarn, which sends a tributary to the Caldew. This tarn is the seat of a singular superstition, being supposed (or perhaps we should say, having been supposed) by the country people to be inhabited by two immortal fish *. Mr. Wordsworth does not tell us in what fairy tale of transformation, or in what other way the belief originated. Saddleback itself is a round-shouldered mountain of great extent, but no beauty of form, except as seen from the south, where the serrated precipices above Threlkeld rival those of Helvellyn. One of these is called Razor Edge, over which there is a magnificent view. Another noticeable point is the top of that wild ravine, down which the great water-spout, many years ago, descended upon Threlkeld, sweeping away part of the village. It is still a strange scene of ruin; and its effect is increased by a singular twist, caused by some convulsion, in the dip of the strata. The view down into Scales Tarn, deep-seated among crags, is awfully grand. In fact Saddleback, though not ascended by one person for ten that go up Skiddaw, is better worth the ascent.

The course of the Greta between Keswick and the foot of Saddleback is very beautiful, and little seen, except by very leisurely travellers. It lies quite in the way of an excursion up Saddleback.

The circuit from Keswick round Bassenthwaite lake is eighteen miles long. About three miles from Keswick the highroad is joined by a bridle-road from Threlkeld to Bassenthwaite, which crosses Latrigg, and goes over the side of Skiddaw, and through the pretty hamlet of Applethwaite. It commands beautiful views of the valley, and is of ready access from Keswick by the bridle-way up Skiddaw. The same road communicates with a peat-track, which goes towards Skiddaw Forest, at a dizzy height along the side of Lonscale Fell, as that offset of Skiddaw is called which presents so bold a front to Saddleback. In dry weather a complete circuit of Skiddaw may be made this way, on horseback, returning by Bassenthwaite. A high wild waterfall, whose name I forget, unmentioned in the guide-books, lies on or near the path, to the north of Skiddaw, where the waters take their first leap out of the forest. Over Water, farther on in the vale of Bassenthwaite, is a marshy uninteresting pool. A rough carriage-road from Keswick to Wigton, distant twenty-two miles, passes through the village of Bassenthwaite, and immediately begins to ascend a steep hill, called Bassenthwaite Hawse, which commands noble views up the vale of the Derwent, and of the Solway, and the hills of Dumfriesshire.

The pyramidal hill which rises to the west of Keswick, above Braithwaite, and over the old Cockermouth road, is called Grisedale Pike. Though only 2680 feet in height, it merits a visit quite as much as Skiddaw, than which it commands, I think, a finer view. Those who love wild scenery will find much pleasure in continuing their walk along the ridge which connects Grisedale Pike with Grassmoor, returning to Keswick over Cawsey Pike, which may very well be done between breakfast and dinner. The views of the Buttermere, Ennerdale, Wastdale, and Borrowdale mountains are extremely good.

It is impossible to fix the time which a tour of the Lakes requires: a fortnight is enough to see the leading features,—three months is not too much to become acquainted with them. Every dale has its peculiar character, and every mountain will repay the trouble of a visit; but there are few, of course, who have time or wish for so minute a survey.

What is the best time of year for a visit to the Lakes?—is another question of interest to the traveller, which it is not easy to answer. Mr. Wordsworth, whose long residence and close observation of the natural phenomena of this land of his choice, entitle his opinion to the highest weight, recommends the space between the middle or last week in May, and the middle or last week in June, in preference to the months of July and August, "as affording the best combination of long days, fine weather, and variety of impressions. Few of the native trees are then in full leaf; but for whatever may be wanting in depth of shade, more than an equivalent will be found in the diversity of foliage, in the blossoms of the fruit and berry-bearing trees which abound in the woods, and in the golden flowers of the broom and other shrubs, with which many of the copses are interveined. In those woods also, and on those mountain-sides which have a northern aspect, and in the deep dells, many of the spring flowers still linger; while the open and sunny places are stocked with the flowers of approaching summer." The disadvantages of July and August are, first, the probability of wet weather, which often sets in with such violence and perseverance as to put all pleasurable expectations to flight; secondly, if the weather be fine, the probability of a long-continued drought, which dries the water-courses, fills the air with haze, and diffuses a leaden uniform colour over everything, which deprives the country of half its beauty. Mr. Wordsworth, page 88, has weighed the objections to the several seasons, and their correspondent advantages: the question is one of the less practical importance, because the period of travelling is seldom left quite free to the traveller's choice. Autumn is certainly the time to see the country to the best advantage; for the mountain-sides glow with a richer colouring than even the woods, when the early frosts have nipped the fern; and before the middle of October it may be confidently expected that some passing storm will robe the hills in snow. But at this time the pedestrian will be liable to be benighted in his longer excursions; and he will have to exchange the pleasure of his twilight strolls for a dull evening over the inn fire. After all, he that carries with him good health and a good temper, cannot go much amiss as to time: one season may be better than another, but each has its peculiar merits as well as demerits. Even the stormiest are most likely to present those occasional revelations of grandeur, which are remembered with delight, heightened rather than impaired, in the retrospect, by the recollection of the inconveniences with which they were purchased *. And not unfrequently, when apparently

* "——Both the undying fish that swim
In Bowscale Tarn did wait on him;
The pair were servants of his eye
In their immortality;
They moved about in open sight,
To and fro for his delight."—
Song at the Feast of Brougham Castle.

* For a description of one of those wonderful atmospherical phenomena, which occur oftenest in stormy weather, see that splendid passage in the 'Excursion,' book ii., near the end:—

——————— "A step,
A single step, that freed me from the skirts
Of the blind vapour, open'd to my view
Glory beyond all glory ever seen
By waking sense or by the dreaming soul.
The appearance instantaneously disclosed
Was of a mighty city—boldly say
A wilderness of building, sinking far
And self-withdrawn into a wondrous depth.
Far sinking into splendour—without end!
Fabric it seem'd of diamond and of gold,
With alabaster domes and silver spires,
And blazing terrace upon terrace high
Uplifted; here serene pavilions bright,
In avenues disposed; there towers begirt
With battlements that on their restless fronts
Bore stars—illumination of all gems!
By earthly nature had the effect been wrought
Upon the dark material of the storm
Now pacified; on them, and on the coves
And mountain-steeps and summits, whereunto
The vapours had receded, taking there
Their station under a cerulean sky."

The passage is continued in the same grand strain to a considerable length.

at the worst, the weather suddenly mends; and on a black rainy morning, when the tourist has been summoning resignation to get through a dull day at his inn, a gleam of light will perhaps shoot through the mist, the clouds begin to break under the influence of the sun, and roll slowly in light fleecy masses up the sides of the mountains. The atmosphere then assumes a transparency and brightness never incident to settled weather, and the landscape is enlivened by a variety of light and shade, and a harmonious contrast of colouring, which can only be enjoyed in a moist climate.

In winter the country fully maintains its character for beauty: I have heard residents of refined taste assert that its superiority over other parts of England is at that season most perceptible. The colouring, though less strongly marked, is hardly less varied than in autumn; and the snow, which commonly robes the higher peaks in spotless white, shaded off into brown and olive as it mixes lower down with the grass and heather, has, in the novelty as well as beauty of its effect, a double charm to the unaccustomed eye. The objections to winter travelling, as a matter of pleasure, are obvious and insurmountable; but those who have occasion to pass near the lakes in mid-winter will be well rewarded for devoting a few days to the becoming acquainted with them under a different aspect. Derwentwater is not unfrequently frozen, and in that state affords to the skater a delightful enjoyment.

We hope next spring to resume this series of articles on British scenery, with some account of the beautiful valleys of the north of Yorkshire; still it will not be irrelevant to devote our small remaining space to a very concise catalogue of those portions of the north of England which may be best seen on the way to and from the Lakes. In approaching them on the west, the whole vale of Lune, from Lancaster to Kirby Lonsdale, the first stage from Kendal towards Leeds, is well worth the attention of those who can deviate from the direct route; especially the Crook of Lune and the neighbourhood of Hornby Castle. Ingleton, the next stage on the way to Leeds, at the foot of Ingleborough, has some curious scenery around it, especially the caves of Yordas, Weathercote, &c. East of Settle, eleven miles from Ingleton, lie Malham Cove and Gordale Scar, two of the most remarkable spots in England, already described in the 'Penny Magazine' for 1833, No. 72. Wharfdale, still more to the east, is beautiful from its source in the moors to Otley and Harewood, a few miles from Leeds. The grounds of Bolton Abbey are the gem of this valley.

The eastern road to Carlisle, by Leeminglane, Stainmoor, and Penrith, skirts a lovely country. There is some pretty scenery between Penrith and Appleby, and the wild road over Stainmoor is striking and pleasant on a fine day. Teesdale, north of the road, from Cross Fell to Wycliff, below Barnard Castle, with its two waterfalls, is perhaps the finest of these Yorkshire valleys. At Greta Bridge, on the high road, lies the well-known scenery of Rokeby. At Catterick Bridge the Swale is crossed, about three miles below Richmond. Swaledale has some pretty scenery, but is inferior to Wensleydale, the next valley to the south, which is traversed by the river Ure, and extends westward nearly to Ingleborough. Aysgarth Force and Jervaulx Abbey are the most remarkable objects in it. Lower down, on the banks of the Ure, near Rippon, stands Fountains Abbey, which needs no praise. Rippon Minster is a fine specimen of our early ecclesiastical architecture. From Rippon there is a double communication with the south, either by Boroughbridge and the York road, or by Harrowgate, Harewood, and Leeds. Knaresborough possesses some objects of curiosity, but to go out of the way for it on the way back from the north would be hardly worth while.

Of the numerous guide-books extant on the subject, Green's 'Guide to the Lakes' is, I believe, inferior to none in accuracy, and superior to all in minuteness of information; it is, however, too bulky for a pocket companion. Mr. Wordsworth's 'Description of the Scenery of the Lakes,' from which we have so largely quoted, is not intended for a guide, but should be read by all persons, for the author's general view of the moral and physical circumstances of the country: it is very short. Baines's 'Companion to the Lakes' is portable and accurate, and lively in its descriptions. But those who want directions and not descriptions, should procure the 'Guide' of Mr. Otley, watchmaker, of Keswick; whose short and sensible notices will send the tourist, without fail, to the things best worth seeing. His pocket-map has been my constant companion, and I can testify to its accuracy, except in one or two points, which have probably been corrected in later editions;—an accuracy really wonderful, considering the smallness of the scale, and such as to render it a trustworthy guide across the hills. From this source, and the 'Geography of the British Islands,' No. I., published by the Society for the Diffusion of Useful Knowledge, the following table of heights has been chiefly formed:—

Above the Sea.	Feet.
Scawfell Pikes	3160
Scawfell	3100
Helvellyn	3070
Skiddaw	3022
Fairfield (Baines)	2950
Gavel	2925
Bowfell	2911
Cross Fell	2901
Pillar	2893
Saddleback	2789
High Street (Baines)	2700
Grassmoor	2756
Grisedale Pike	2680
Coniston Old Man	2577
Harrison Stickle } Langdale Pikes	2400
Pike of Stickle } Langdale Pikes	2000
Carrock Pike	2290
Cawsey Pike	2040
Black Comb	1919
Honistar Crag (Baines)	1700
Catbells	1400
Pass of Sty Head	1250
Pass of Kirkstone (Baines)	1200
Latrigg	1160
Loughrigg Fell (Baines)	1050
Dunmail Raise (Baines)	720

In Yorkshire.	
Wharnside	2385
Ingleborough, rather less	
Pendle Hill	1803

Height of Lakes Above the Sea.	
Red Tarn (Helvellyn)	2400
Sprinkling Tarn (Borrowdale)	1900
Hawes Water	714
Thirlmere	473
Ulswater	460
Derwentwater	288
Crummock Water	260
Bassenthwaite Water	210
Esthwaite Water	198
Grasmere	196
Wastwater	160
Windermere	116
Coniston Water	105

*** The Office of the Society for the Diffusion of Useful Knowledge is at 59, Lincoln's Inn Fields.

LONDON: CHARLES KNIGHT & CO., 22, LUDGATE STREET.

Printed by WILLIAM CLOWES and SONS, Stamford Street.

Artists and Engravers

The Charles Knight Collection

OLD LONDON

Artists and Engravers

HENRY C. ANDREWS was a botanical artist and engraver. He also published several books on flora and fauna undertaking the complete task himself as author, illustrator and engraver. His main contribution to Charles Knight's books was as an engraver. He exhibited at the Royal Society of British Arts between 1839 and 1856. His only contribution in this series is as the engraver of 'KNIGHTSBRIDGE – ONE MILE FROM LONDON.'

*

HENRY ANELAY was a landscape painter and illustrator. As well as his contributions to Charles Knight's journals he also provided numerous plates for the Illustrated London News.' He exhibited at the Royal Academy between 1858 and 1873. Examples of his work can be seen in this book in 'KNIGHTSBRIDGE' and 'THE ELEPHANT AND CASTLE' where his skill is seen at its best.

*

THOMAS BEWICK was not a contributor to Charles Knight's books but he had a tremendous influence on the improvement in the quality and style which emerges in the mid nineteenth century box wood engravings. His clear cut style lived on after his death in 1828 and is characterised in the work of Charles Knight's Chief Engraver, John Jackson who studied and was apprenticed under Bewick in Newcastle before moving to London.

*

FREDERICK FAIRHOLT was a distinguished illustrator and engraver. As an artist he specialised in Heraldry and Buildings and won a Society of Arts medal in his early teens. He learnt his engraving skills whilst working with one of Charles Knight's assistant engravers – S. Sly. He travelled widely and was the artist of many of Charles Knight's overseas scenes that appear in 'Penny Magazine' and other journals. He died in London in 1866. His fine work is seen in 'OLD ROYAL EXCHANGE' in this book.

*

JOHN GRIEG's work can be seen in the Hyde Park Gates scene in the frontpiece of 'PICTURE OF LONDON' shown in the introduction of this book. He was highly skilled in all aspects of and was a draughtsman, engraver, lithographer as well as an accomplished landscape painter.

*

JOHN SMITH HEAVISIDE studied under Bewick in Newcastle before moving to London. As well as contributing to Knight's works he illustrated Parker's archaeological books. He died in London in 1864. He was the engraver of Anelay's drawing of the 'ELEPHANT AND CASTLE.'

*

JOHN JACKSON was Charles Knight's Chief Engraver between 1832 and 1845. He was a pupil of the master of nineteenth century box wood engraving Thomas Bewick and was responsible for the vast improvement in the quality of reproduction and the transcription onto stereotypes. He was the engraver of many of the works in Knight's books including the Penny Magazines, London and Old England. His contribution to this book includes 'BLACKFRIARS BRIDGE', 'SEVEN DIALS', 'CORN EXCHANGE', 'POST OFFICE' and our Premier picture 'WREN'S TOWERS AND SPIRES.'

*

HARDEN SIDNEY MELVILLE was an artist of extreme talent and specialised in landscapes, animals and sport exhibiting between 1837 and 1882 at the Royal Academy and the Royal Society of British Artists. He travelled widely and was the artist of many of the Europe and overseas sketches in the 'Penny Magazines.' His splendid drawing of 'LONDON BRIDGE' is taken from an original sketch by John Norden in 1616 and the Visscher landscape of London (1615).

*

AMBROSE POYNTER's work can be seen in his magnificent parallel drawing of 'WREN'S TOWERS AND SPIRES.' Among his many talents he was an Architect, Landscape Painter and Illustrator who designed government schools and churches. He became a founder member of the RIBA in 1834 and was a pupil of John Nash. He exhibited at the Royal Academy but sadly from 1858 to his death in 1888 he was blind and gave up his artistic work.

*

THOMAS HOSMER SHEPHERD specialised in the drawing of city buildings. As well as being the artist for many of Charles Knight's rquirements he undertook commissions for drawings of Bath, Bristol, Edinburgh, Athens and London interiors between 1827 and 1842. He exhibited at the Royal Society of British Artists. They were praised for their "outstanding skill and beauty" and we can see this quality in his drawings in this book which are THAMES TUNNEL, WARWICK LANE, ST. JOHN'S GATE and ST. JAMES'S PARK.

*

S. SLY was originally a topographer but was employed by Charles Knight to study under John Jackson as an assistant engraver. He emulated his master's skills and is responsible for many of the engravings in Knight's wide range of publications. His contribution in this book is the engraving of ISLINGTON GREEN.

*

HENRY TIFFIN was a prominent artist and landscape painter who exhibited at the Royal Academy and the British Institution between 1840 and 1874. His particular skill for detail was complemented by the comment of Charles Knight that he '... brought London to life through his drawings.' This can clearly be seen by his illustrations in this book – 'BLACKFRIARS BRIDGE, 'SEVEN DIALS', 'THE POST OFFICE', and the 'CORN EXCHANGE.'

*

Other contributors to Charles Knight's LONDON include Murdon, Smyth, Mead, Sargent, Sears, Green, Rembault and Jarvis.

*

Illustrations Index

* PM refers to Penny Magazine section.

Obituary to Charles Knight

Gateway to Bachelors' Acre Burial Ground, Windsor

THE ILLUSTRATED LONDON NEWS

THE ILLUSTRATED LONDON NEWS MARCH 22, 1873

THE LATE CHARLES KNIGHT.

Our news last week recorded the death of this veteran publisher and editor, sound English scholar and original author, who laboured during half a century, with results most beneficial to his country, in the creation of a cheap and good popular literature. The son of a bookseller at Windsor, born in 1791, and educated in a private school at Ealing, he began, at twenty-one, to conduct a local newspaper, the *Windsor and Eton Express*, to which he added the *Plain Englishman*, a monthly miscellany of entertainment, published in that town. In 1820 he took the editorship of the *Guardian*, a London weekly paper; but soon left this to set up the *Etonian*, a monthly magazine which received contributions from the cleverest young men of that great public school; and some of them, Macaulay, Praed, Moultrie, Derwent and Nelson Coleridge, were the supporters of *Knight's Quarterly Magazine*, his next venture. All this was preparatory to the main work of his life.

The Society for the Diffusion of Useful Knowledge was a literary and educational phase of the great Whig Reforming party, some forty-five years ago. Its performances, in the judgment of the social historian, did nearly as much good to the nation as was done by all their political achievements when in power. Henry Brougham, Lord Althorp, Lord John Russell, Sir John Cam Hobhouse, and Mr. Spring Rice, with other noblemen and gentlemen of influence, lent their countenance to the efforts of its zealous committee. Amongst them were Rowland Hill and Matthew Hill, Captain Francis Beaufort, Herman Merivale, James Mill and Henry Hallam, Bishop Maltby, Sir Isaac Goldsmid, Mr. J. W. Lubbock, Mr. Leonard Horner, Messrs. William Tooke, William Allen, and Zachary Macaulay, Sir Charles Bell, Dr. Roget, and Dr. Elliotson, men of distinguished talents and usefulness in various ways. "The Library of Entertaining Knowledge," a series of cheap volumes which treated of history, antiquities, and natural science in a pleasing descriptive style, was one of the earliest products of their co-operation. The *Quarterly Journal of Education* was the organ of their views. Charles Knight joined the society in 1827, and in the next year brought out, under its auspices, the *British Almanac and Companion*, which was and is a most convenient yearly hand-book of information, physical, statistical, and official or legislative, for reference upon all subjects arising out of the course of the seasons, or events of the year. His next work for the society was to compose, in 1831, several little treatises on "The Rights of Industry," "Capital and Labour," and "The Results of Machinery," which came out successively under the title of "The Working Man's Companion." These essays, sold for a shilling, were calculated to help in settling the vexed problems of that time.

But it was in the *Penny Magazine*, commenced on Saturday, March 31, 1832, a few weeks after *Chambers' Edinburgh Journal*, that Charles Knight, publisher for the Useful Knowledge Society, set a very important example. We have the first two years' volumes now before us. Each weekly number consists of eight pages, all of clear large print, with five or six wood engravings. Many of these engravings, presented in the early numbers of the Magazine, had previously done duty in the "Library of Entertaining Knowledge." But others were designed and executed for this penny sheet, under the direction of the late Mr. John Jackson. Until the commencement of the ILLUSTRATED LONDON NEWS, ten years later, the *Penny Magazine* was the best attempt made to combine the art of engraving on wood with the compilation of a literary periodical for the popular taste. The subjects which the *Penny Magazine* illustrated by these means were of various kinds; famous pictures and statues, from the British and Continental galleries of art; scenes of landscape or costume and manners in foreign countries; objects of antiquarian interest, specimens of natural history, and various curiosities, in the British Museum; rare animals in the Zoological Society's Gardens; cathedrals, palaces, castles, and other noble buildings; places of renown in any country, for historical events that happened there; the processes of agriculture and manufactures, with shipping, fisheries, and mines; besides, what was especially attractive, the portraits of illustrious men, of all nations and ages, with a biographical memoir of each person, given on the anniversary of his birthday. The descriptive, narrative, or expository comments were usually written by contributors who were more or less conversant with the class of topics intrusted to them; and some of these writers afterwards developed their special knowledge to a fuller extent in the *Penny Cyclopædia*. All this solid instruction was mingled with short extracts from interesting new books, select pieces of poetry, and translations from the Greek and Latin classics, whereby the ancient heroes and mythological deities were brought side by side with the utilitarian inventions of the nineteenth century. The general effect of such a miscellany was highly stimulating to the intellectual curiosity of those who were mere boys and girls at that time, but who are now middle-aged men and women. They will cherish a fond remembrance of the *Penny Magazine* to the end of their lives. It differed in some respects from the Edinburgh publication of William and Robert Chambers, or the more recent *Household Words* of Charles Dickens, which were offered, the former at three-halfpence, the latter at twopence. These contained, from the first, not only humorous or serious original essays, upon minor questions of moral or social interest, but tales and fictitious sketches of life. The *Penny Magazine*, for its part, relied mainly upon the interest of facts; it had a cheerful practical eye to the present, a sedately historical regard for the past, and the sensational baits of fancy were rather eschewed. Political and theological partisanship was strictly excluded. Nevertheless, the sale reached 160,000 copies, printed by Mr. William Clowes, as we learn from an account of the printing machinery and its operation in December, 1833. There were times when the sale, weekly and monthly, amounted to 200,000. The *Penny Magazine* enjoyed great prosperity during several years, but declined after a time under other management than Charles Knight's. He had, in January, 1833, commenced, at his own risk, the *Penny Cyclopædia* (afterwards remodelled by the original projector, first as the "National," and then as the "English Cyclopædia")—a work on which he expended more than £40,000 for literature and engravings. It was not a commercial success; but Mr. Knight has since explained that it would have paid a handsome profit had it not been for the enormous sum which he paid to the Government in the form of paper duty—a sum amounting on the whole work to £16,500. At the end of the twenty-seventh volume, which completed letter Z, he found that, although he had a sale of about 20,000 copies throughout, his loss on the Cyclopædia was between £20,000 and £30,000. Mr. Knight, by his pamphlets, "The Struggles of a Book against Excessive Taxation," and "The Case of the Authors as regards the Paper Duty," has, doubtless, contributed in no small degree to the repeal of the taxes on knowledge.

The close, in 1844, of Charles Knight's connection with the Useful Knowledge Society, which had occupied the "second epoch" of his life, since his unsuccessful start, in 1824, in Pall-mall East, as an independent publisher, left him already engaged in several great literary undertakings on his own account. He had brought out the "Pictorial Bible," edited by Dr. Kitto, from 1836 to 1838; the "Pictorial Shakspeare," from 1839 to 1841, inclusive; the "London," commenced in 1841, to which Mr. Saunders, Mr. Fairholt, and Mr. Planché gave their literary assistance; above all, "The Pictorial History of England," chiefly written by the late Mr. Charles Macfarlane and Mr. G. L. Craik, but with some aid from the writers just named, and from Sir Henry Ellis, Mr. Andrew Bisset, Mr. W. Weir, and (for the history of art) Mr. E. J. Poynter. This last-mentioned work, continued during seven years, was one of national interest; and we should hope that the public will not be indifferent to an appeal recently made for relief to the impoverished daughters of Mr. Macfarlane, who was an industrious and meritorious person. As for Charles Knight, the time had not yet come for him to write a History of England with his own pen. He was busy at this period with his Shakspeare studies, and with the issue of different serial publications, designed for the household reading of those who cannot buy expensive books. Six volumes of a "Library for the Times," and "The Store of Knowledge for all Readers," in 1841, with "Miscellanies" of the same date, were followed by "Knight's National Library of Select Literature," and next by "Knight's Weekly Volume," sold at one shilling, for which he wrote, in 1844, the biography of Caxton; and for this too he edited a selection of pieces from "The Lowell Offering," the productions of American factory-girls, under the title of "Mind Amongst the Spindles." In the list of his own writings for such mixed collections of old and new matter are a treatise upon "The Elephant, Viewed in Relation to Man," and a "Sketch of the Commercial Intercourse of the World with China;" for nothing came amiss to him that was useful or rationally interesting. But Shakspeare and English history, with English topography, were decidedly the subjects of his mental predilection. During more than twenty years he spent all his leisure in gathering and arranging materials for the treatment of these favourite themes. In the "third epoch" of his active career, to the end of 1862, he was enabled to perform what he had designed for their elucidation.

The value of Charles Knight's labours as a Shakspearean critic and commentator has, perhaps, been a little depreciated since the appearance of the "Cambridge Shakspeare," as well as the scholarly editions of Mr. Dyce and Mr. Staunton. The "Pictorial Shakspeare," which was a beautiful work of graphic illustration, was but the first effort he made in this line of editorship, sustained by patient researches in a spirit of reverent affection for the greatest English poet, and, if not with infallible judgment, yet always with fine natural taste. He produced many editions of Shakspeare in different forms, after the "Pictorial," completed in 1842; the "National" in 1851, the "Companion Shakspeare" in 1852, and the "Stratford Shakspeare" in 1853, for which he wrote a judicious biography of Shakspeare; also the "Cabinet Shakspeare," jointly with Mr. Robert Chambers, in 1856. "Studies and Illustrations of Shakspeare," in 1850, and another volume of "Studies," had previously appeared. In 1853, upon the alleged discovery, by Mr. Payne Collier, of a corrected copy of the "old folio," Charles Knight came to the rescue of the commonly received text in a pamphlet called "Old Lamps or New?" There was a new issue of his "Pictorial Shakspeare" in 1864; and he produced the "Blackfriars" and two other cheap editions between 1866 and 1868. With respect to the next grand object of his literary industry, the topographical description of his native country, Charles Knight in like manner proceeded to carry on what he had begun in the pictured pages of "London." He followed up this, in 1845, with "Old England; a Pictorial Museum of National Antiquities." After retiring from the business of official publisher to the Poor-Law Board, he travelled frequently in different parts of Great Britain and Ireland, seeing much that was turned to good account in his work on "The Land We Live In," which came out in 1848. The preparation of these and other pleasant volumes of a similar kind was an agreeable help towards his third and most considerable task of original authorship—the "Popular History of England." This was intended to supply the want complained of by Lord John Russell in a speech at Bristol in 1854, when that statesman observed that "we have no other history of England than that of Hume to give to a young man of age to think for himself." This work treats "not only of Kings, Courts, and Cabinets, but of the people, their habits and ways, and modes of thought; not only of wars by land and sea, but of social legislation, of popular ideas, their growth and development; of popular rights and their assertion." It embraces the progress of agriculture, manufactures, and commerce, of literature and the arts, the manners and household life of different classes. It was published in serial parts, of which the first appeared in 1855, and the last at the end of 1862. Charles Knight wrote also for Miss Martineau's "History of the Thirty Years' Peace" a preliminary narrative, on the same plan, of events during the first fifteen years of the nineteenth century. An abridgment of his "Popular History of England," for the use of schools, was published in 1865.

Such are the principal works of this true-hearted, faithful, diligent English man of letters, who has so well earned the grateful esteem of his countrymen. He has told the story of his life in a delightful autobiography, which shows much of the social history of this and the last generation. We have certainly not yet enumerated nearly all the books that he produced, either written or compiled by his own hand or composed under his editorial direction. There were many charming essays—"Once upon a Time," "Rambles by Rivers," and "Shadows of Old Booksellers." Was it worth while to speak of juvenile effusions—a tragedy called "Arminius, or the Deliverance of Germany," in 1814; "The Bridal of the Isles, a Masque," and "Blighted Hopes, a Monody," or of "The Brazen Head," a magazine of witty squibs, partly furnished by Praed? All clever young men of a literary turn have attempted such flights of genius. Charles Knight went into regular harness, served the printer's and publisher's business needs, and did a noble stroke of really useful work. That "Cyclopædia," which was one of his best gifts to the public, spoilt, indeed, the making of his private fortune. But he has made a good name—that of a good scholar, a good author, a good man. Douglas Jerrold used to say that his epitaph should be two words, simply these—"Good Knight!"

He was buried in Old Windsor churchyard, on Friday week, attended by many of his friends. The Portrait we give is from a photograph by Mr. Jabez Hughes, of Ryde, which has been taken in deference to the opinion of some members of the family, though it seems rather to show Charles Knight in the infirmity of his last few years, than such as he was at the time when he still conversed freely with the world. Almost the latest public incident of his life was to receive the offer of an honorary membership of the "Historical Society of Great Britain," through its secretary, the Rev. Dr. C. Rogers; but this compliment was declined on account of Mr. Knight's state of health; he was nearly blind some time before his death.

Mr [illegible]

3 Clifton Road, St John's Wood, N.W.
September 8, 1859.

Sir,

Upon sending yesterday for a single volume — Brown's Estimate — my messenger was asked "Have you brought any back?" The question appears to me somewhat unnecessary; for, with the exception of Wright's History of the House of Hanover, I have no book belonging to the London Library which has been a week in my possession. If any of the books I have are called for, I shall be obliged by receiving the usual note. Those I took out on Friday, the 2d are as follows:— King's Anecdotes 1 vol. Cavendish [illegible] Chatham 4 v. Grenville 4 v. Aiken 2v. I presume that I am not expected to read them at the new-novel speed.

I remain Sir
Respectfully Yours
Charles Knight

A letter written by Charles Knight to the British Library.

Epilogue

Epilogue

In the process of writing this book and selecting the eighteen pictures to form the OLD LONDON Charles Knight Collection we soon realized the enormity of the task to give true justice in recognition of Charles Knight. As research progressed it became clear that the man was a forgotten genius in so many respects – some of his achievements have been identified in this book – but so much more needs to be said and shown.

There are many other engravings in the Charles Knight volumes we would have wished to include and more superb written descriptions of and about OLD LONDON which could not be incorporated. It is clear that in time we too should produce further volumes but in this closing section we show some of the illustrations which were left out of our first OLD LONDON Collection. 'Smithfield by Torchlight' and 'West Cheap Conduit' were our 'first reserve' choices and are shown on the opposite page.

As we have progressed the response and interest by the many people we have contacted has encouraged us to investigate and research further to find specific engravings related to places, activities or cultural interests appropriate to the needs of individuals and organisations. We have therefore used some additional designs to assist various charities in their fund raising efforts. These drawings can be seen on subsequent pages and include:

TEMPLE BAR	An engraving by John Jackson, Charles Knight's Chief Engraver, from Hogarth's famous work '5th November Celebrations'. This design was selected by the Society for the Prevention of Asbestosis and Industrial Diseases.
SOUTHWARK CATHEDRAL	From a drawing by J.W. Archer the delightful scene of the Cathedral from the south was engraved by John Jackson. Known as St. Mary Overies until it gained cathedral status in 1905 the building is closely associated with Chaucer, Dickens and William Shakespeare. The design was selected by 'The Friends of Southwark Cathedral'.
THE GLOBE	This engraving of Shakespeare's Globe was originally drawn for Charles Knight's Pictorial Edition of Shakespeare's Works which was produced in eight volumes during the early 1840's. It would seem that the drawing was based on an original by Visscher of about 1618. This is one of the designs selected by the Shakespeare Globe Trust to assist in the fund raising efforts for the completion of the new Globe complex on London's Southbank due to be opened on the anniversary of Shakespeare's birth – 23 April 1993.

Every aspect of research on Charles Knight reveals something new. On visiting the British Library we found that 132 entries are recorded in the BL Catalogue amounting to well over 400 volumes. Historians in Windsor revere the achievements of their townsman but the Memorial Gate is in disrepair and threatened with demolition as a result of new development plans. The bust of Charles Knight which used to stand proudly in the Guildhall has been relegated to the museum store but we are informed that it will be reinstated during an exhibition in 1991 to commemorate the Bicentenary of Charles Knight's birth.

One of the more unusual aspects of our discoveries was uncovered whilst researching the differing content in the numerous editions of Charles Knight's LONDON. For instance it was only the first 1840 edition that contained an introduction and the 'title' engravings of Westminster, City and Old London used at the start of this book. Charles Knight was the publisher of the first edition but whether it was due to some financial aspect or personal consideration reprints were undertaken by other publishers. Based on research for what he termed 'Entertaining London' he later wrote a more academic 'History of London' which was published in the early 1860's. Some were pictorial editions using the same wood engravings prepared for 'Penny Magazines', 'London' and other earlier publications.

The same principal applied when he prepared and published 'OLD ENGLAND' between 1843 and 1845. Obviously it was good economic practice to reuse engravings for different publications and all those prepared for 'LONDON' also appeared in his superb two volumes of 'OLD ENGLAND' which we mentioned in the introduction to this book. Once again he arranged for others to publish the reprints – James Sangster of Paternoster Row in London and he later authorised a further publication of 'OLD ENGLAND' in the United States of America which was produced by Samuel Walker and Co. of Boston in about 1856.

In this book we have obviously concentrated on LONDON but Charles Knight saw 'London' in a much wider context. It was after all the capital of England and the Empire. Eventually his books and journals reached every corner of the English speaking world. We are viewing his achievements as a London publisher and the impact and contribution he made for his Country. It seems appropriate therefore to include some engravings of other parts of England which were brought to the awareness of Victorian Londoners for the very first time through his weekly journals 'The Land we Live In' and 'Railway Rambles'. Having written and illustrated England's heritage he encouraged the City inhabitants to use the new modes of transport available to them and go into the Country and see for themselves!

The historic towns were mainly featured and some of these including Canterbury, York, Worcester and Chichester are illustrated here. As Charles Knight said '. . . these eminent towns and cities report and serve our Capital in a Regal, Ecclesiastical, Municipal and Baronial context – for where does London begin and London end?'. This is precisely where Charles Knight starts his volumes of OLD ENGLAND and it is our intention to recognise the Bicentenary year of Charles Knight's birth by producing a similar volume to 'Charles Knight's LONDON' which will not unreasonably be called 'Charles Knight's OLD ENGLAND'.

In the early 1840's London was an extraordinary mixture of industrial and rural existence. Charles Knight's artists and engravers captured such scenes through a magnificent series of illustrations of 'London at Work' and 'Nature'. These appeared in the 'Penny Magazines' and included in this final section are 'The Hat Factory' and 'The Sugar Refinery' representing activities in the industrial sector. At this time Sheep, Cows and Deer were commonly seen in the fields within a short distance of Central London and some of these animals are shown through the fine work of John Jackson.

One of the London establishments Charles Knight used for his research was the British Museum and he refers constantly to his 'finds'. Some which he believed identified the true epitome of past London – and indeed past England were the illuminated Anglo-Saxon manuscripts which he found in the Cotton Library within the museum. It was only recently that we appreciated the significance of these references. In the first chapter of the first volume on LONDON Charles Knight refers to William Fitz-Stephen's record of the Anglo Saxon period called 'Description of London'. Part of this represents a Calendar written in Latin and Anglo Saxon and illustrated with characteristic employments of each month of the year. These have been beautifully engraved for Charles Knight volumes and we show those of 'January' and 'November'.

* * *

When I visited Simon Hughes at the House of Commons offices in Whitehall to discuss the final aspects of this book I realized that unwittingly I had come a full circle. The 'View of Old London' which we had treasured and were surprised could be reproduced to the quality which is illustrated at the beginning of this book was there in the main reception but seen from a different angle and perspective. It was a large coloured engraving looking northwards across London and is in fact a facsimile of a picture called LONDON, WESTMINSTER AND SOUTHWARK 1543 by Ante Van Den Wyngrerde. The original picture is part of the Sutherland Collection which is held in the Bodeleian Library at Oxford. It is now clear that this is the painting from which the artist of 'View of Old London' based his drawing and it also enables us now to date that Old London scene precisely.

Had that visit not taken place then we may never have realised the true significance and origin of the fascinating picture which appeared as an introduction to Charles Knight's LONDON. I am also grateful to Simon for his kind agreement to write the Foreward of this book and his critique from which some final alterations were made. His enthusiasm and support has been a great encouragement.

There is only one way to end a book in which I feel I have been more of a compiler than an author. If, as I hope, you have enjoyed the wonderful way in which Charles Knight portrayed his London then that is where the credit rightly rests and we therefore close in the most appropriate way by what he described as 'The Silent Highway':

> There, indeed is the river, still flowing and still ebbing, – the most ancient thing we can look upon, – which made London what it was and what it is. Nearly all that then adorned its banks has perished; and many of the stirring histories of the busy life that moved upon its waters have become to us as obscure as the legend of 'New Troy'.

W.J. TIFFIN. DEL.
J.JACKSON.S.

Temple Bar

Southwark Cathedral

Shakespeare Portraits

The Globe Theatre

St. Augustine's Gate, Canterbury

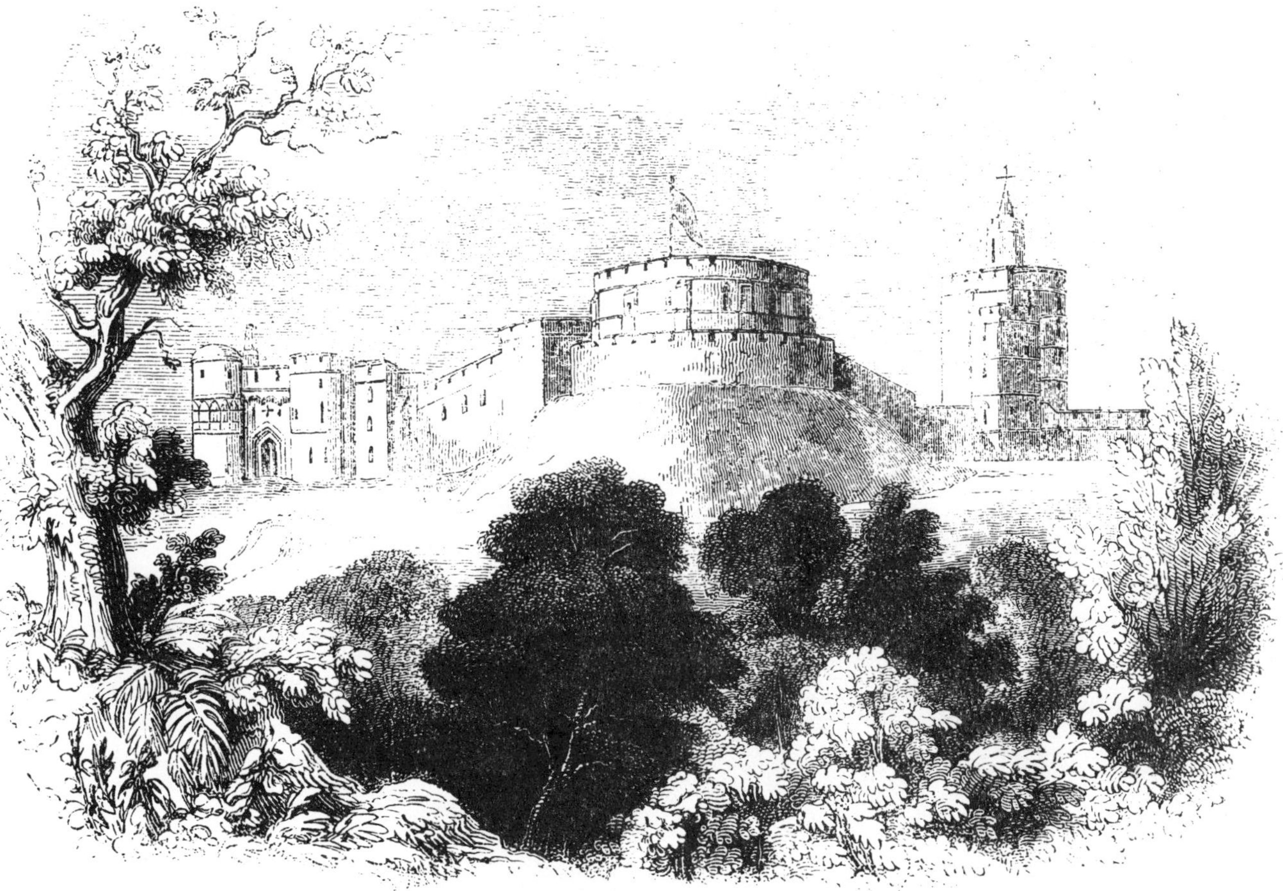

Windsor Castle at time of Edward III

York

Oxford (Botanical Gardens)

The Hat Factory

The Sugar Refinery

Chichester

Worcester

[Long or Middle-Horned Cattle.—*a*, Old Craven Bull ; *b*, Shropshire Ox ; *c*, New Leicester Bull; *d*, Devon Bull; *e*, Devon Cow ; *f*, Hereford Bull; *g*, Hereford Cow ; *h*, Sussex Cow.

English Cattle

[The Red Deer, or Stag, and the Roe-Deer.]

Deer of the British Islands

Saxon Emblems of the Month of January.

Saxon Emblems of the month of November.

General Index

* PM refers to Penny Magazine section